THE TREATS™ TRUCK

BAKING BOOK

THE TREATS™ TRUCK

BAKING BOOK
cookies, brownies & goodies galore!

KIM IMA

WILLIAM MORROW

An Imprint of HarperCollins*Publishers*

HarperCollins books may be purchased for educational, business, or sales promotional use.
For information please write: Special Markets Department, HarperCollins Publishers,
10 East 53rd Street, New York, NY 10022.

FIRST EDITION

Designed by Austyn Stevens
Photography by Jason Florio

Library of Congress Cataloging-in-Publication Data

Ima, Kim.
  The Treats Truck baking book : cookies, brownies and goodies galore!
/ Kim Ima. — 1st ed.
      p. cm.
   ISBN 978-0-06-206577-3
 1. Pastry. 2. Treats Truck (Street vendor) 3. Cookbooks. I. Title.
  TX773.I43 2011
  641.8'65 — dc23
                                          2011015317

11 12 13 14 15 ID / RRD 10 9 8 7 6 5 4 3 2 1

To our customers,

you are the best in the world
and dear to my heart

CONT

Hi!

TODAY'S SPECIAL IS: really really good!

yum!

ENTS

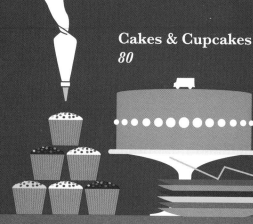

One day in the middle of a conversation with a dear friend about cookies (we both love cookies), I suddenly had an idea, "The Treats Truck!" I cried out. I could see it. I could see it coming around the corner at the same time I could imagine me as the driver. And, of course, I could imagine a truck filled with treats.

"What's not to like about that?" my friend agreed.

"I want to make it real," I told my friend. It was love. And when it's love, what else can you do? Find a truck, learn how to drive in the city, learn how to make your favorite brownie recipe, times ten, and open for business.

I believe in treats. I do. I believe in those little moments in the middle of an ordinary day when you treat yourself or a friend to a cookie.

The best part of having The Treats Truck is our customers. Their pleasure and excitement at the truck makes it all worthwhile at the end of the day. Isn't that what a treat is all about? Making someone's day? I believe that treats find their way into every person's heart (and stomach). They remind us of home, of being a kid, of our families and friends. They're a simple thing—a simple thing that's fun to make, fun to eat, and really, really fun to share.

I hope you enjoy this book and have a great time baking with it. And when you're in New York City, stop on by our truck or come to our bakery in Brooklyn, The Treats Truck Stop. We'd love to see you.

Kim
(owner/baker/driver)

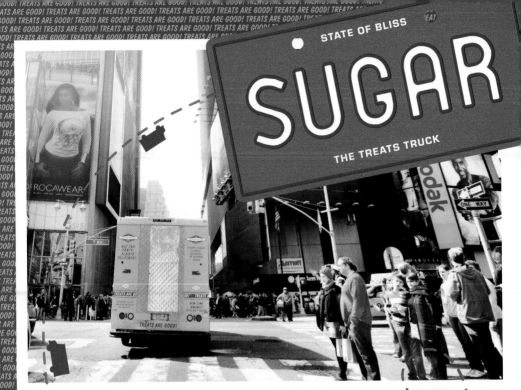

The Treats Truck Is My Bakery on Wheels.

HIS NAME IS SUGAR.

Each day, we bake in Brooklyn and our truck, Sugar, heads out to all our favorite neighborhoods! Some treats are especially popular in certain spots. Peanut-butter-and-jelly sandwich cookies for Midtown Manhattan! Cran-almond crispies and cupcakes for Park Slope, Brooklyn! The Upper West Side loves sugar cookies with sprinkles and caramel cremes!

What will be your favorite?

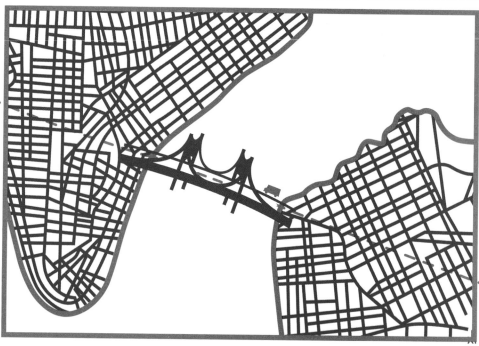

BAKING TIME!

I love baking. Whether on your own, with a friend, or with kids by your side, baking is such a pleasurable way to spend some time, and it's hard to beat a plate of freshly baked treats on your kitchen counter, for the stomach and for the heart. At The Treats Truck Stop, we bake a lot of treats. We specialize in old-fashioned, homey desserts. We have daily Specials, sometimes taking one of our favorite standards and giving it a little twist. You can do the same at home—I like to call it the Mix & Match. Take cookies, cakes, and brownies and match them with frostings, fillings, and toppings to create lots of different kinds of treats. *So, here we go!*

For storing cookies, generally I recommend placing them in an airtight container on your counter. Most cookies can be stored this way for 3 to 5 days or even longer. Keep brownies and bars wrapped or in containers, as well. Many people I know also like to freeze cookies and brownies occasionally, whether they have baked them at home or bought them from us. Then you can take out one or two at a time and keep the rest fresh. For pies and cakes, I think it's best to keep them well covered in a cool dry spot in your kitchen or in the refrigerator, depending on the kind of frosting or filling. A slice of pie or a piece of cake a day or two after you first serve it is such a satisfying snack, don't you agree?

RECIPES! TIPS! BAKE, MIX, MATCH, AND ENJOY!

Our recipes use good old-fashioned ingredients, like unsalted butter, sugar (white, dark brown, and confectioners'), whole milk, all-purpose flour, large fresh eggs, good chocolate, pure vanilla extract, and a whole lot of sprinkles. An electric mixer is quite useful, although in a pinch, brute manpower and a whisk will do. And we'll give you suggestions for stocking your kitchen with all the basic tools you'll need. Most are probably already in your kitchen!

BAKING WITH FRIENDS? Prep the recipe ahead of time for easy assembly and clean-up while you go—or even prepare the dough ahead of time, so you can get right down to the fun of baking and frosting! As fun as it is to make and enjoy baked goods, I also really believe they color some of our best memories of time with our families and friends. They help us mark special occasions and give us a lift on an otherwise ordinary day. I'm especially drawn to *not too fancy recipes* that are easy to make at home. That's what I grew up on, and that's what is most fun for me to make.

QUICK STORY. One day, a regular customer and her daughter came by the truck with a sandwich bag of oatmeal cookies they had just baked. The daughter, about four, was so excited to give them to me. "She's been talking about this for weeks," the woman told me. "She kept saying that you bake for everyone, so someone should bake for you."

Here's to baking!

TREATS ARE GOOD! TREATS ARE GOOD! TREATS ARE GOOD! TREATS ARE GOOD! TREATS ARE GOOD! TREATS ARE GOOD! TREATS ARE GOOD! TREATS ARE GOOD! TREATS ARE GOOD! TREAT
REATS ARE GOOD! TREATS ARE GOOD! TREATS ARE GOOD! TREATS ARE GOOD! TREATS ARE GOOD! TREATS ARE GOOD! TREATS ARE GOOD! TREATS ARE GOOD! TREATS ARE GO
EATS ARE GOOD! TREATS ARE GOOD! TREATS ARE GOOD! TREATS ARE GOOD! TREATS ARE GOOD! TREATS ARE GOOD! TREATS ARE GOOD! TREATS ARE GOOD! TREATS ARE GOOD! TREATS.
GOOD! TREATS ARE GOOD! TREATS ARE GOOD! TREATS ARE GOOD! TREATS ARE GOOD! TREATS ARE GOOD! TREATS ARE GOOD! TREATS ARE GOOD! TREATS ARE GOOD! TREATS ARE GOOD!

TIPS, TOOLS & MEASUREMENTS!

BAKE JUST A FEW COOKIES ANYTIME YOU PLEASE!

Make dough, prescoop or roll out and cut your cookies, wrap well, and keep in the fridge or freezer.

PREHEAT! PREHEAT! PREHEAT!

KNOW YOU'RE GOING TO BE BAKING LATER AND WANT TO CUT STEPS?

Measure out your dry ingredients into containers and set aside.

FOR MOST RECIPES, BUTTER AND EGGS ARE BEST AT ROOM TEMPERATURE.

½ STICK = ¼ CUP = 4 TABLESPOONS = 2 OUNCES

1 STICK = ½ CUP = 4 OUNCES
2 STICKS = 1 CUP

BUTTER IS GOOD!

MIX WELL BUT DO NOT OVERMIX!

ROLL DOUGH UNDER WAX PAPER OR PARCHMENT FOR LESS STICKING.

SPOON FLOUR GENTLY INTO A MEASURING CUP,

then level the cup with a knife.

USE PLASTIC OR GLASS MEASURING CUPS FOR LIQUIDS.

USE PLASTIC OR STAINLESS STEEL FOR DRY INGREDIENTS.

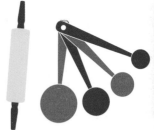

READ A RECIPE CAREFULLY AHEAD OF TIME.
Have everything you need? Need to factor in time for chilling dough or making frosting?

BE PRECISE WITH THE BASIC RECIPE, BUT FEEL FREE TO PLAY WITH ADD-INS AND SPECIAL TOUCHES—BAKING IS A SCIENCE AND AN ART!

EVERY OVEN IS A LITTLE DIFFERENT. GET TO KNOW YOURS AND HOW IT BAKES.

Measurements

DASH	⅛ TEASPOON
3 TEASPOONS	1 TABLESPOON
2 TABLESPOONS	1 OUNCE
4 TABLESPOONS	¼ CUP
5 TABLESPOONS & 1 TEASPOON	⅓ CUP
1 CUP	8 OUNCES
2 CUPS	16 OUNCES (1 POUND)

FAVORITE TOOLS AROUND THE KITCHEN:

- Baking sheets
- 9 by 9-inch square baking pan
- 9 by 13-inch baking pan
- Cupcake/muffin pans
- Medium saucepan
- Big mixing bowl
- Big pot
- Rolling pin
- Stand mixer or hand mixer
- Butter knife
- Fork
- Wooden spoon
- Whisk
- Regular spatula
- Small containers with lids for storage
- Sturdy plastic storage bags *(great to use as piping bags)*
- Lemon zester
- Grater
- Ice cream scoop
- Mesh strainer (or sifter)
- Timer

HIGHLY RECOMMENDED ADDITIONS:

- Parchment paper
- Small offset spatula
- Bowl scraper
- Silicone spatula
- Long offset spatula
- Small pastry brush
- Piping bag and tips
- Two 9-inch round cake pans
- 9-inch springform pan
- Wire cooling rack

COOKIES

Cookies might just be one of the best inventions on earth. A cookie can really brighten up a day or be the best gift ever— it's the perfect little snack with a glass of milk or a cup of tea or a really good cup of coffee.

Baking cookies has always been a favorite pastime of mine. When I was a kid, it was one of the first activities that felt kind of grown-up but also like playtime— measuring the ingredients, mixing the dough, trying not to sneak too many tastes, peeking in the oven door, waiting, just waiting, to see the cookies come out of the oven. Then waiting again—the torturous few minutes more for the cookies to cool before reaching over to take one or two or three. The delight and pleasure of a well-spent hour in the kitchen baking cookies is still hard to beat.

Here are some of our favorite cookie recipes at The Treats Truck, including childhood faves like chocolate chip and sugar cookies! We start you off with small batches, so we encourage you to double or triple them to please a big hungry crowd or if you want to freeze dough or cookies for later. And we also encourage you to play with the size of the cookies. Big, little, or somewhere in between, cookies of all sizes are fun for different occasions!

CHOCOLATE CHIPPERS

Chocolate chip cookies. What can I say? They are a favorite, a classic! And one of the most popular to bake at home. Everyone has a favorite style of chipper, from soft to crispy. I like them when they're a little crispy on the edges and soft in the center. You can adjust the baking time to get them just right for you. And, while they are great to bake anytime you please, I think they should be a requirement for any rainy afternoon!

INGREDIENTS

1 CUP (2 STICKS) BUTTER, SOFTENED

1 CUP FIRMLY PACKED DARK BROWN SUGAR

⅜ CUP WHITE SUGAR

1 EGG

2 TEASPOONS VANILLA EXTRACT

2⅓ CUPS FLOUR

1 TEASPOON BAKING SODA

1 TEASPOON BAKING POWDER

1 TEASPOON SALT

1 TO 1½ CUPS SEMISWEET OR MILK CHOCOLATE CHIPS

Makes 1½ to 3 dozen cookies, depending on how big you make them

1   Preheat the oven to 350°F.

2   In a large bowl, cream the butter and sugars together until light and fluffy. Add the egg and vanilla and mix well.

3   In a medium bowl, combine the flour, baking soda, baking powder, and salt.

4   Gradually add the flour mixture to the butter mixture, mixing well as you go. Stir in the chocolate chips.

5   Scoop the dough into round drops (big or little, you decide!) with a spoon or an ice cream scoop and place them 2 inches apart on a baking sheet.

6   Bake for 9 to 12 minutes, or longer as needed or desired. Remember that the cookies will continue to bake a bit after they come out of the oven. If you like them soft or crispy, you may vary the time accordingly.

7   Let the cookies cool (if you can resist!) before moving them from the baking sheet.

TREATS ARE GOOD! TREATS ARE GOOD! TREATS ARE GOOD! TREATS ARE GOOD! TREATS ARE GOOD! TREATS ARE GOOD! TREATS ARE GOOD! TREATS ARE GOOD! TREATS ARE GOOD! TRE
RE GOOD! TREATS ARE GOOD! TREATS ARE GOOD! TREATS ARE GOOD! TREATS ARE GOOD! TREATS ARE GOOD! TREATS ARE GOOD! TREATS ARE GOOD! TREATS ARE G
TREATS ARE GOOD! TREATS ARE GOOD! TREATS ARE GOOD! TREATS ARE GOOD! TREATS ARE GOOD! TREATS ARE GOOD! TREATS ARE GOOD! TREATS ARE GOOD! TREA
E GOOD! TREATS ARE GOOD! TREATS ARE GOOD! TREATS ARE GOOD! TREATS ARE GOOD! TREATS ARE GOOD! TREATS ARE GOOD! TREATS ARE GOOD! TREATS ARE GO

PEANUT BUTTER COOKIES

INGREDIENTS

2 EGGS

**2 TEASPOONS
VANILLA EXTRACT**

**2 CUPS SMOOTH
PEANUT BUTTER
(WITHOUT ADDED
SUGAR)**

1 CUP SUGAR

½ TEASPOON SALT

These peanut butter cookies are delicious, and this is the best peanut butter recipe and one of the simplest! Also, it's gluten-free, which is great for those people with wheat restrictions. But most of our customers love them purely for their peanut buttery goodness, especially when they're made into peanut butter sandwich cookies!

Makes 2½ to 3 dozen cookies

1   Preheat the oven to 325°F. Grease a baking sheet or line it with parchment paper.

2   In a small bowl, combine the eggs and vanilla. Set aside.

3   Place the peanut butter in a large bowl and pour in the egg-vanilla mixture. Stir with a sturdy spoon or mix with your hands (really, it's a great technique!) until combined.

4   Add the sugar and salt and mix well.

5   Scoop the dough with a spoon and roll it into balls with your hands. The size of the scoop of dough is up to you, depending on the size cookies you prefer (the dough doesn't spread much). Place the balls 2 inches apart on the baking sheet. Pat the balls flat and use a fork to make crosshatch marks on the top of each cookie.

6   Bake for about 10 minutes, or until the centers look as light and baked as the edges. Cool completely before removing from the cookie sheet with a spatula.

Mix&Match with

Peanut Butter
Filling to make
Peanut Butter
Sandwich Cookies
(page 28)

**VARIATION:
ADD CHOCOLATE
CHIPS TO MAKE
A YUMMY PEANUT
BUTTER CHOCOLATE
CHIPPER!**

SUGAR DOT SUGAR COOKIES

On The Treats Truck, we call our frosted sugar cookies sugar dots (made with a 1³/₈-inch cookie cutter) and big sugar dots (made with a 2½-inch cookie cutter). Little sugar dots are just the right size for a little kid, or for a grown-up who just wants a tiny cookie. Our customers often buy a dot or two to tag along with whatever bigger treat they pick out! In addition to big and little dots, we love seasonal and holiday-shaped cookie cutters for making sugar cookies. Who doesn't love a ghost cookie at Halloween or a snowman cookie in winter? Hearts for Valentine's Day and flowers for the spring!

INGREDIENTS

Makes 1½ to 3 dozen cookies, depending on how big you make them

3 CUPS FLOUR

1½ TEASPOONS BAKING POWDER

½ TEASPOON SALT

1 CUP (2 STICKS) BUTTER, SOFTENED

1 CUP SUGAR

1 EGG, SLIGHTLY BEATEN

3 TABLESPOONS HEAVY CREAM

1 TEASPOON VANILLA EXTRACT

1 In a medium bowl, combine the flour, baking powder, and salt. Mix and set aside.

2 Use a mixer to cream the butter and sugar until light and fluffy.

3 Add the egg and mix well.

4 In a measuring cup, combine the heavy cream and vanilla.

5 Mix the flour mixture into the butter-sugar mixture in three parts, alternating with the cream and vanilla mixture, starting and ending with the flour.

6 Remove the dough from the bowl, form it into a block, and wrap it in plastic wrap. Refrigerate for at least 1 hour and up to overnight.

7 Preheat the oven to 350°F.

8 With a rolling pin, roll out the dough to ¼ inch thick. Using a cookie cutter, cut out the cookies and place them 1 inch apart on a greased or parchment paper–lined baking sheet.

9 Bake for 10 to 12 minutes, or until oh-so-lightly golden at the edges.

10 Allow the cookies to cool completely. Frost with buttercream frosting and sprinkles or the topping of your choice!

Mix&Match with

Buttercream Frosting (page 60),

Meringue Wash (page 76) & Sprinkles (page 78),

Peppermint Frosting (page 66), or

Chocolate Espresso Filling/Topping (page 65)

FROSTING & DECORATING YOUR SUGAR COOKIES!

You can either frost the cooled cookies right away or store the unfrosted cookies until you're ready to frost them. Give the frosted cookies at least 30 minutes to set before moving them—but sampling one right away is encouraged! You can also decorate sugar cookies with just sprinkles or sanding sugar, with the help of a meringue wash (page 76).

LEMONY LEMON DOT COOKIES

Mix&Match with

Lemony Lemon Frosting (page 62) and

sprinkles (I like white or rainbow nonpareils for these)

On the truck, we like to frost sugar cookies with lemon frosting and call them Lemony Lemon Dots. The combination of the sugar cookie and the lemon frosting is really lovely.

Bake the size and shape sugar cookies you desire. After the cookies have cooled, frost with lemony lemon frosting. Top with sprinkles, if you'd like!

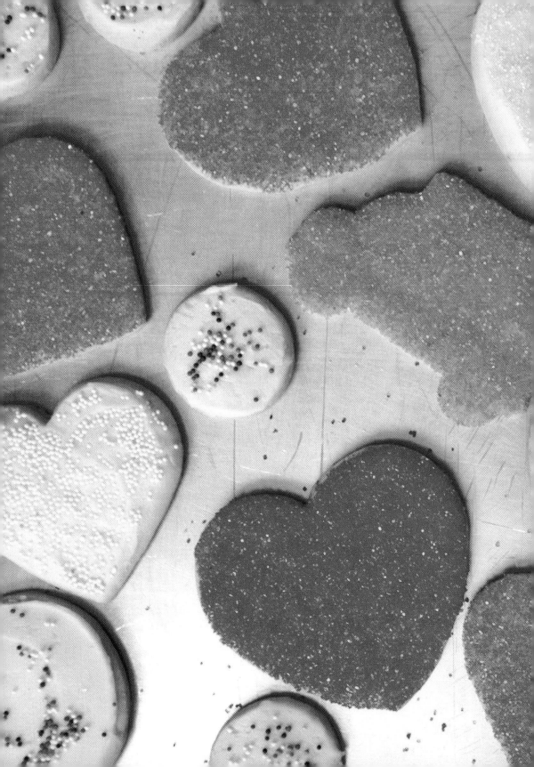

OATMEAL COOKIES

OLD-FASHIONED, PLAIN JANE, AND OATMEAL CHOCOLATE CHIPPERS

INGREDIENTS

1 CUP (2 STICKS) BUTTER

1 CUP PACKED DARK BROWN SUGAR

⅛ CUP WHITE SUGAR

2 EGGS

2 TEASPOONS VANILLA EXTRACT

1½ CUPS FLOUR

1 TEASPOON BAKING SODA

1 TEASPOON GROUND CINNAMON

1 TEASPOON SALT

3 CUPS OLD-FASHIONED OATS

When I think of an old-fashioned oatmeal cookie, I think oatmeal with raisins. I've also been a lifelong believer in a good oatmeal chocolate chip, and then there are those times when a totally plain oatmeal cookie—a Plain Jane, I call it—really hits the spot. Start with the basic oatmeal cookie recipe and add as you wish.

Makes about 1½ dozen cookies (or double the recipe for a big batch!)

1   Preheat the oven to 350°F. Grease a baking sheet or line it with parchment paper.

2   In a large bowl, cream the butter and sugars together until light and fluffy. Add the eggs, one at a time, and mix well. Stir in the vanilla.

3   In a separate bowl, combine the flour, baking soda, cinnamon, and salt.

4   Gradually add the flour mixture to the butter mixture, mixing until fully incorporated.

5   Mix in the oats and any add-ins you fancy!

6   Use a spoon or an ice cream scooper to scoop up balls of dough. Place them about 2 inches apart on the baking sheet.

7   Bake for 12 to 14 minutes, or until golden at the edges.

OPTIONAL ADD-INS: 1 to 1½ cups raisins, chocolate chips, chopped pecans, walnuts, dried cranberries, minced dried cherries, currants—whatever you like!

TREATS ARE GOOD! TREATS ARE GOOD! TREATS ARE GOOD! TREATS ARE GOOD! TREATS ARE GOOD! TREATS ARE GOOD! TREATS ARE GOOD! TREATS ARE GOOD! TREATS ARE GOOD! TR
RE GOOD! TREATS ARE GOOD! TREATS ARE GOOD! TREATS ARE GOOD! TREATS ARE GOOD! TREATS ARE GOOD! TREATS ARE GOOD! TREATS ARE GOOD! TREATS ARE GOOD! TREATS ARE GOOD! TREATS
TREATS ARE GOOD! TREATS ARE GOOD! TREATS ARE GOOD! TREATS ARE GOOD! TREATS ARE GOOD! TREATS ARE GOOD! TREATS ARE GOOD! TREATS ARE GOOD! TREATS ARE GOOD! TRI
GOOD! TREATS ARE GOOD! TREATS ARE GOOD! TREATS ARE GOOD! TREATS ARE GOOD! TREATS ARE GOOD! TREATS ARE GOOD! TREATS ARE GOOD! TREATS ARE GOOD! TREATS ARE G

OATMEAL JAMMYS

INGREDIENTS

OATMEAL COOKIE
DOUGH (PAGE 10)

JAM (OR JAMS!)
OF YOUR CHOICE

On The Treats Truck, we serve a lot of oatmeal jammys, the oatmeal version of a thumbprint cookie. Our favorite jams to use are raspberry and apricot.

Makes about 1½ dozen cookies (or double the recipe for a big batch!)

1   Preheat the oven to 350°F.

2   Place scoops of oatmeal cookie dough 2 inches apart on a greased or parchment paper–lined cookie sheet. Use your thumb to make a hollow in the dough.

3   Use a piping bag or a spoon to put a dollop of jam in the center of each cookie.

4   Bake for 12 to 14 minutes, or until the cookies look fully baked and the edges are golden.

WE RECOMMEND USING A THICK JAM. THE JAM WE USE IS VERY THICK AND DELICIOUS.
Did we mention we love jam?

CHOCOLATE COOKIES & CHOCOLATE CHOCOLATE CHIPPERS

INGREDIENTS

2 CUPS FLOUR

**1 CUP PLUS
1 TABLESPOON
UNSWEETENED
COCOA POWDER**

1¾ CUPS SUGAR

**⅜ TEASPOON
BAKING SODA**

½ TEASPOON SALT

**2 STICKS PLUS
2 TABLESPOONS
BUTTER, CUBED
AND SOFTENED**

**5 TABLESPOONS
MILK**

**1½ TEASPOONS
VANILLA EXTRACT**

This recipe is the base we use for both chocolate cookies and chocolate chocolate chippers. The basic difference is that chocolate cookies are rolled and cut out, while the slightly plumper chocolate chocolate chippers are drop cookies loaded with chocolate chips. And chocolate cookies can be used to make sandwich cookies or even crumbled up to make a cookie piecrust (page 110)!

Makes about 40 cookies

1   Preheat the oven to 350°F and grease a baking sheet or line it with parchment paper.

2   In a large bowl or mixer, combine the flour, cocoa powder, sugar, baking soda, and salt.

3   Add the butter and mix until a dough forms.

4* Add the milk and vanilla and mix until the dough is smooth.

5   Mold the dough into one big block, wrap it in plastic wrap or put it in a container, and refrigerate it for at least 30 minutes to overnight.

6   Roll out the dough to about ¼ inch thick. Cut out cookies with a round cookie cutter (or any shape you like). Place the cookies at least 1 inch apart on the baking sheet.

7   Bake for 8 to 10 minutes. If the cookies look a little soft when you take them out, don't worry! They'll firm up as they cool. Cool in the pan or move after a few minutes to a wire rack.

*CHOCOLATE CHOCOLATE CHIPPERS:

Mix in 1 cup chocolate chips after **step 4**. Scoop the dough with a spoon and form a ball of dough with your hands. Place the balls of dough on the cookie sheet and press down gently to flatten each cookie. Add a few extra chocolate chips to the top when no one is looking. Bake for 10 to 12 minutes, or until set but still soft—and enjoy!

COCONUT MACAROONS

INGREDIENTS

6 EGG WHITES

6 TABLESPOONS SUGAR

1½ TEASPOONS VANILLA EXTRACT

¾ TEASPOON ALMOND EXTRACT

4½ CUPS SHREDDED SWEETENED COCONUT

Old-fashioned macaroons are a big hit with our customers. We serve them year-round, although they especially remind me of Passover dinners at my grandparents' house. Some customers get particularly excited about them because they're gluten-free.

Makes 12 to 14 large macaroons

1   Preheat the oven to 350°F. Grease a baking sheet or line it with parchment paper.

2   In a large bowl, combine all the ingredients and mix using your hands or with a fork.

3   Using a 2-inch scoop or a large spoon, scoop the mixture into balls and place them 1 inch apart on the baking sheet.

4   Bake for 14 to 16 minutes, or until lightly toasted on top.

VARIATION: ADD CHOCOLATE CHIPS BEFORE BAKING TO MAKE CHOCOLATE CHIP MACAROONS!

NOT TOO FANCY, ALWAYS DELICIOUS!™

CINNAMON COOKIES

INGREDIENTS

½ CUP (1 STICK) BUTTER

1 CUP SUGAR

1 EGG

1 TEASPOON VANILLA EXTRACT

1½ CUPS FLOUR

1½ TEASPOONS BAKING POWDER

¼ TEASPOON SALT

1 TEASPOON CINNAMON

These cookies are perfect with tea or a tall glass of milk. You can leave them plain or frost them with cinnamon frosting!

Makes about 2 dozen cookies

1   In a large bowl, cream the butter and sugar together.

2   Add the egg and vanilla and mix well.

3   In a separate bowl, combine the flour, baking powder, salt, and cinnamon.

4   Add the flour mixture to the butter mixture and mix until thoroughly combined.

5   Pat the dough into a large mound and wrap in plastic wrap or put it in a covered container. Refrigerate the dough for at least 30 minutes to overnight.

6   Preheat the oven to 350°F and grease a baking sheet or line it with parchment paper.

7   Roll the dough to about ¼ inch thick. Cut out cookies with a round cookie cutter, or any shape you wish. Place the cookies 1 to 2 inches apart on the baking sheet.

8   Bake for 10 to 14 minutes, or until set but still soft.

Mix&Match with

Cinnamon Frosting (page 68)

PUMPKIN SWIRL COOKIES

These cookies are a favorite around Thanksgiving time. They're a nice complement to all the pies on the dessert table and a great snack anytime. They're a bit more labor-intensive than most of our recipes, but they're so well worth it! And if you've prepared the dough ahead of time, you can keep it in the freezer ready to slice and bake, as easy as pie.

Makes 2½ to 3 dozen cookies

INGREDIENTS

DOUGH

2 CUPS FLOUR

½ TEASPOON GROUND CINNAMON

¼ TEASPOON BAKING POWDER

¼ TEASPOON SALT

¾ CUP (1½ STICKS) BUTTER, SOFTENED

1¼ CUPS WHITE SUGAR

1 EGG

¼ TEASPOON VANILLA EXTRACT

¼ TEASPOON ALMOND EXTRACT

FILLING

1 CUP CANNED PUMPKIN PUREE

1 TEASPOON PUMPKIN PIE SPICE

¼ CUP PACKED DARK BROWN SUGAR

GLAZE

3 TABLESPOONS CANNED PUMPKIN PUREE

2 TABLESPOONS BUTTER, MELTED

1¼ CUPS CONFECTIONERS' SUGAR

1 TEASPOON GROUND CINNAMON

¼ TEASPOON GROUND ALLSPICE

TREATS ARE GOOD! TREATS ARE GOOD! TREATS ARE GOOD! TREATS ARE GOOD! TREATS ARE GOOD! TREATS ARE GOOD! TREATS ARE GOOD! TREATS ARE GOOD! TREATS ARE GOOD! TREATS ARE GOOD! TREATS ARE G
EATS ARE GOOD! TREATS ARE GOOD! TREATS ARE GOOD! TREATS ARE GOOD! TREATS ARE GOOD! TREATS ARE GOOD! TREATS ARE GOOD! TREATS ARE GOOD! TREATS ARE GOOD! TREATS ARE GOOD! TREATS ARE GOOD!
RE GOOD! TREATS ARE GOOD! TREATS ARE GOOD! TREATS ARE GOOD! TREATS ARE GOOD! TREATS ARE GOOD! TREATS ARE GOOD! TREATS ARE GOOD! TREATS ARE GOOD! TREATS ARE GOOD! TREATS ARE GOOD! TREATS ARE GO

1

TO MAKE THE DOUGH, using a fork, whisk, or sifter, mix the flour, cinnamon, baking powder, and salt in a large bowl and set aside.

2

In a bowl or mixer, cream the butter and sugar.

3

In a small bowl, mix the egg, vanilla, and almond extract.

4

Pour the egg mixture into the butter/sugar mixture and mix until combined. Gradually add the flour mixture and mix just until the ingredients are incorporated. Don't overmix—you want the dough to be stiff but not tough.

5

Roll the dough between a piece of folded parchment paper or wax paper to create a 12 by 9-inch rectangle. Place the wrapped dough flat on a baking sheet and freeze until firm, about 15 minutes.

6

TO MAKE THE FILLING, mix the pumpkin puree, pumpkin spice, and brown sugar together in a small bowl.

7

TO ASSEMBLE, peel the top layer of parchment paper from the dough. Spread a thin layer of filling over the entire rectangle of dough. You should still be able to see the dough through the filling. You may not need all the filling.

8

Starting on a long side of the rectangle, roll up the dough like a cake roll. Wrap the roll tightly in the parchment paper, place it seam side down on the baking sheet, and freeze for at least 1 hour.

9

Preheat the oven to 375°F and line a baking sheet with parchment.

10

Remove the parchment from the roll of dough and carefully cut the roll into ¼-inch-thick slices. Place the cookies 2 inches apart on the baking sheet.

11

Bake for 8 to 10 minutes, or until the edges start to turn golden brown. Let cookies cool on the baking sheet.

12

TO MAKE THE GLAZE, combine the pumpkin puree and butter. Add the confectioners' sugar, cinnamon, and allspice and mix well.

13

If you want to be fancy, put the glaze in a small piping bag and decorate the cookies with a dashing squiggle or curlicue! Or, just use a butter knife to spread a swish of glaze across the top.

EATS ARE GOOD! TREATS ARE GOOD! TREATS ARE GOOD! TREATS ARE GOOD! TREATS ARE GOOD! TREATS ARE GOOD! TREATS ARE GOOD! TREATS ARE GOOD! TREATS ARE GOOD! TREATS ARE GOOD! TREATS ARE GOOD!
E GOOD! TREATS ARE GOOD! TREATS ARE GOOD! TREATS ARE GOOD! TREATS ARE GOOD! TREATS ARE GOOD! TREATS ARE GOOD! TREATS ARE GOOD! TREATS ARE GOOD! TREATS ARE GOOD! TREATS ARE GOOD! TREATS ARE
EATS ARE GOOD! TREATS ARE GOOD! TREATS ARE GOOD! TREATS ARE GOOD! TREATS ARE GOOD! TREATS ARE GOOD! TREATS ARE GOOD! TREATS ARE GOOD! TREATS ARE GOOD! TREATS ARE GOOD! TREATS ARE GOOD!

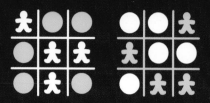

GINGERSNAPS

INGREDIENTS

¾ CUP (1½ STICKS) BUTTER

¼ CUP PACKED DARK BROWN SUGAR

½ CUP WHITE SUGAR

¼ CUP UNSULFURED MOLASSES (SEE NOTE)

1 EGG

½ TEASPOON VANILLA EXTRACT

2 CUPS FLOUR

1 TEASPOON BAKING SODA

¼ TEASPOON SALT

1½ TEASPOONS GROUND CINNAMON

2 TEASPOONS GROUND GINGER

½ TEASPOON GROUND CLOVES

½ CUP WHITE SANDING SUGAR (PAGE 78)

Makes about 45 one-inch balls, but feel free to make them any size you'd like

1   In a bowl or mixer, cream the butter and sugars. Add the molasses, egg, and vanilla and stir until thoroughly mixed.

2   In a separate bowl, combine the flour, baking soda, salt, cinnamon, ginger, and cloves.

3   Add the flour mixture to the butter mixture and mix until combined.

4   Cover the bowl or wrap the dough in plastic wrap and refrigerate it for 30 minutes to overnight.

5   Preheat the oven to 350°F. Grease a baking sheet or line it with parchment paper.

6   Scoop out the dough with a spoon and roll it into 1- to 2-inch balls with your hand (whatever size you prefer!).

7   Pour the sanding sugar into a small bowl or plate.

8   Roll the dough balls in the sugar and place the cookies 2 inches apart on the baking sheet. Press the cookies down as thin as you want, using your hands or the side of a glass as a mini-rolling pin. The thinner the cookie, the crisper it will be.

9   Bake for 12 to 15 minutes. The longer you bake the cookies, the more they'll crisp up. Cool on the baking sheet or move to a wire rack.

I love both gingersnaps and gingerbread cookies. What's the difference? The ingredients are similar, but gingersnaps do come out crisper, especially if you make them thin, and gingerbread cookies are perfect for rolling out and cutting into shapes, such as gingerbread men. Here are the recipes for both kinds!

The recipes for both gingersnaps and gingerbread cookies call for molasses. I recommend using a light, unsulfured molasses. You can also use dark molasses if you prefer, keeping in mind that the flavor will be stronger and the cookies a bit darker.

GINGERBREAD COOKIES

INGREDIENTS

½ CUP (1 STICK) BUTTER, SOFTENED

½ CUP SUGAR

1 EGG

⅔ CUP UNSULFURED MOLASSES

3 CUPS FLOUR

½ TEASPOON SALT

¾ TEASPOON BAKING SODA

2 TEASPOONS GROUND GINGER

1 TEASPOON GROUND CINNAMON

½ TEASPOON GROUND CLOVES

Mix & Match with

Royal Icing
(page 76)

Gingerbread cookies, especially gingerbread men, really add to the holiday spirit each December. Whether you celebrate Christmas or not, they're a wonderful seasonal treat!

Makes about 40 three-inch gingerbread men

1 In a large bowl, cream the butter and sugar. Stir in the egg and molasses until combined.

2 In a separate bowl, combine all the dry ingredients. Add the dry ingredients to the butter mixture and mix until combined.

3 Wrap the dough in plastic wrap and refrigerate for at least 30 minutes to overnight.

4 Preheat the oven to 350°F. Grease a baking sheet or line it with parchment paper.

5 On a lightly floured surface, use a rolling pin to roll out the dough to your desired thickness (I usually roll it to about ¼ inch thick). Use cookie cutters to cut the cookies into any shapes you desire—from plain circles to gingerbread men!

6 Bake for 8 to 10 minutes, or until firm.

7 Cool the cookies for 1 minute on the sheet, and then move to fully cool on a wire rack before decorating with royal icing.

SANDWICH COOKIES

TREATS ARE GOOD! TREATS ARE GOOD! TREATS ARE GOOD! TREATS ARE GOOD! TREATS ARE GOOD! TREATS ARE GOOD! TREATS ARE GOOD! TREATS ARE GOOD! TREATS ARE GOOD! TREATS ARE GOOD!

TREATS ARE GOOD! TREATS ARE GOOD! TREATS ARE GOOD! TREATS ARE GOOD! TREATS ARE GOOD! TREATS ARE GOOD! TREATS ARE GOOD! TREATS ARE GOOD!

*Okay, so we have kind of a
sandwich cookie obsession
at The Treats Truck. There's
just something about
a sandwich cookie. . . .*

*Two cookies with extra good
stuff in between? What's not
to like about that?*

You'll find all our favorite sandwich cookies here. Try our recipes, then feel free to create your own. Your friends, family, and neighbors will be very, very happy to help you taste-test any new cookie creations you whip up.

Another fun thing to keep in mind—you can make any size sandwich cookie you'd like! We use a round 2¼-inch round cookie cutter for our standard size caramel cremes and Truckers, a 1½-inch round cutter for our small ones, and a 1¼-inch round cutter for the mini-ones—as well as a round 2½-inch cookie cutter for our raspberry rings. **Whatever size—all a delight!**

CARAMEL CREME SANDWICH COOKIES

INGREDIENTS

COOKIES

1½ CUPS FIRMLY PACKED BROWN SUGAR

2 CUPS (4 STICKS) BUTTER

2 EGG YOLKS

4 CUPS FLOUR

FROSTING

½ CUP (1 STICK) BUTTER

2 TEASPOONS VANILLA EXTRACT

5 CUPS CONFECTIONERS' SUGAR

6 TABLESPOONS MILK

These brown sugar cookies with a browned butter frosting in the middle are one of my favorites. They're old-fashioned and a little unfamiliar to a lot of people. But browned butter frosting sounds good, doesn't it? It's really, really good!

Makes about 28 sandwich cookies

1   TO MAKE THE COOKIES, in a large bowl, cream the sugar and butter. Add the egg yolks and flour and mix well.

2   Wrap the dough in plastic wrap and refrigerate for at least 30 minutes, to overnight.

3   Preheat the oven to 325°F. Grease a baking sheet or line it with parchment paper.

4   Use a rolling pin to roll the dough to ¼ inch thick. Cut out the cookies using a round cookie cutter. If the dough seems too soft, refrigerate the rolled-out dough for a bit to firm it up before cutting the cookies.

5   Place the cookies 1 inch apart on the baking sheet and bake for 10 to 12 minutes, or until ever-so-slightly golden. Set aside on the baking sheet to cool completely.

6   TO MAKE THE FROSTING, in a medium pan over medium heat, brown the butter, stirring often until small brown flecks appear. Take off the heat.

7   Add the vanilla and confectioners' sugar and whisk to combine. Whisk in the milk, 1 tablespoon at a time, until the mixture is creamy and smooth. If the frosting seems too thick, add a little more milk. (You can keep the frosting in a covered container in the fridge if you make it ahead of time or aren't quite ready to use it. When you're ready to fill the cookies, give the frosting time to soften a bit, or stick it in the microwave for 10 seconds or a bit more.)

8   Using an offset spatula or a butter knife, frost the underside of 1 cookie and top with a second cookie to make a sandwich. If you prefer, use a piping bag or a plastic storage bag with the tip cut off to place a dollop of frosting on the upturned cookie and then top with the second cookie. Repeat with the rest of the cookies. The cookies will keep in an airtight container for 3 to 5 days.

CINNAMON SANDWICH COOKIES

Mix&Match

Cinnamon Cookies (page 15) or Sugar Dot Sugar Cookies (page 6) with

Cinnamon Frosting (page 68)

Spread a layer of frosting on the underside of a cookie with a butter knife or small offset spatula or pipe a dollop of frosting with a piping bag—your choice! Place a second cookie on top to make a sandwich.

OPTIONAL: Add sanding sugar (see page 78) with meringue wash (see page 76) for a sparkly top.

TREATS ARE GOOD! TREATS ARE GOOD! TREATS ARE GOOD! TREATS ARE GOOD! TREATS ARE GOOD! TREATS ARE GOOD! TREATS ARE GOOD! TREATS ARE GOOD! TREATS ARE GOOD! TRE
GOOD! TREATS ARE GOOD! TREATS ARE GOOD! TREATS ARE GOOD! TREATS ARE GOOD! TREATS ARE GOOD! TREATS ARE GOOD! TREATS ARE GOOD! TREATS ARE GOOD! TREATS ARE
TREATS ARE GOOD! TREATS ARE GOOD! TREATS ARE GOOD! TREATS ARE GOOD! TREATS ARE GOOD! TREATS ARE GOOD! TREATS ARE GOOD! TREATS ARE GOOD! TREATS ARE GOOD! TRE
GOOD! TREATS ARE GOOD! TREATS ARE GOOD! TREATS ARE GOOD! TREATS ARE GOOD! TREATS ARE GOOD! TREATS ARE GOOD! TREATS ARE GOOD! TREATS ARE GOOD! TREATS ARE GO

CHOCOLATE TRUCKERS

Mix&Match

Chocolate Cookies
(page 12) with

Buttercream
Frosting (page 60)

Our Chocolate Trucker is a sandwich cookie made with chocolate cookies and buttercream frosting. The only problem with Truckers is that they seem to disappear rather quickly and mysteriously when you leave a plate of them out on a table.

1   If you're using a piping bag, fill it two-thirds full with buttercream frosting. I like to use a star tip, but any tip will work. If you're not using a piping bag, use a butter knife or small offset spatula.

2   Place a chocolate cookie upside down and put a nice dollop of frosting on the cookie. Place another chocolate cookie on top to make a sandwich. Press down gently to push the frosting out a bit. It's so pleasing to see the frosting plump out to the edges of the cookies.

3   Let the sandwich cookies set for at least 15 minutes before stacking or placing in a container. The cookies, well wrapped or in an airtight container, will keep for 2 to 4 days.

SPECIALS ARE GOOD! SPECIALS ARE GOOD! SPECIALS ARE GOOD! SPECIALS ARE GOOD! SPECIALS ARE GOOD! SPECIALS ARE GOOD! SPECIALS ARE GOOD! SPECIALS ARE GOOD! SPECIALS ARE GOOD! S
SPECIALS ARE GOOD! SPECIALS ARE GOOD! SPECIALS ARE GOOD! SPECIALS ARE GOOD! SPECIALS ARE GOOD! SPECIALS ARE GOOD! SPECIALS ARE GOOD! SPECIALS ARE GOOD! SPECIALS ARE GOOD! SP
SPECIALS ARE GOOD! SPECIALS ARE GOOD! SPECIALS ARE GOOD! SPECIALS ARE GOOD! SPECIALS ARE GOOD! SPECIALS ARE GOOD! SPECIALS ARE GOOD! SPECIALS ARE GOOD! SPECIALS ARE

TRUCKER SPECIALS

We have a number of kinds of Truckers we feature as Specials.
Mix and match to your heart's delight!

DOUBLE CHOCOLATE TRUCKERS

MINT CHOCOLATE TRUCKERS

PEANUT BUTTER CHOCOLATE TRUCKERS

Mix&Match
Chocolate Cookies (page 12) with

Chocolate Ganache (page 64) and chocolate jimmies or finely chopped or shaved chocolate (optional)

Mix&Match
Chocolate Cookies (page 12) with

Mint Chocolate Filling (page 65) and finely chopped mint chocolate, chopped dark chocolate, or chocolate jimmies (optional)

Mix&Match
Chocolate Cookies (page 12) with

Peanut Butter Filling (page 69)

Spread chocolate ganache on the underside of a cookie, then place a second cookie on top to make a sandwich. Press lightly so that the filling can be seen between the cookies. If you like, roll the edges of the cookies in chocolate jimmies or finely chopped chocolate.

Spread mint chocolate filling on the underside of a cookie, then place a second cookie on top to make a sandwich. Press lightly so that the filling can be seen between the cookies. If you like, roll the edges of the cookies in finely chopped mint chocolate, chopped dark chocolate, or chocolate jimmies.

With a spoon or your fingers, scoop a spoonful of the peanut butter filling and place it on the underside of a cookie, then place a second cookie on top to make a sandwich. I like to use my hands to make a little "peanut butter patty," as if I were making a little hamburger on a bun.

ALS ARE GOOD! SPECIALS ARE GOOD! SPECIALS ARE GOOD! SPECIALS ARE GOOD! SPECIALS ARE GOOD! SPECIALS ARE GOOD! SPECIALS ARE GOOD! SPECIALS ARE GOOD! SPECIALS AR
S ARE GOOD! SPECIALS ARE GOOD! SPECIALS ARE GOOD! SPECIALS ARE GOOD! SPECIALS ARE GOOD! SPECIALS ARE GOOD! SPECIALS ARE GOOD! SPECIALS ARE GOOD! SPECIALS ARE
SPECIALS ARE GOOD! SPECIALS ARE GOOD! SPECIALS ARE GOOD! SPECIALS ARE GOOD! SPECIALS ARE GOOD! SPECIALS ARE GOOD! SPECIALS ARE GOOD! SPECIAL

PEANUT BUTTER SANDWICH COOKIES

Peanut butter sandwich cookies are very popular at all of our spots, but especially in Midtown Manhattan! And this recipe is gluten-free, which is great for our customers who have gluten restrictions. These cookies can be stored in an airtight container in the refrigerator for 3 to 5 days. You can also wrap them well and freeze them. When you take the cookies out of the freezer, just unwrap them and set them aside to defrost. I have one customer who buys two dozen at a time and takes out one a day before lunch to have later for his midafternoon treat!

PEANUT BUTTER PEANUT BUTTER

Mix&Match
Peanut Butter Cookies (page 5) with

Peanut Butter Filling (page 69)

With a spoon or your fingers, scoop a spoonful of peanut butter filling and place it on the underside of a cookie. I like to use my hands to make a little "peanut butter patty," as if I were making a little hamburger on a bun. If you're making a PB&J, spread jam on a second cookie. Top with the second cookie to make a sandwich.

PB&J

Mix&Match
Peanut Butter Cookies (page 5) with

Peanut Butter Filling (page 69) and the jam of your choice

I love the mix of peanut butter and brown sugar in our peanut butter filling, but peanut butter straight from the jar also works.

FEEL FREE TO TRY BOTH!

PEANUT BUTTER & CHOCOLATE

Mix&Match
Peanut Butter Cookies (page 5) with

Chocolate Filling (page 64)

Spread or spoon a healthy dollop of chocolate filling on the underside of a cookie. Top with a second cookie to make a sandwich. Let the cookies set for a while or put them in the fridge to give the chocolate a chance to firm up. But eat one right away if you please, of course!

OATMEAL CREAMWICH COOKIES

Mix&Match
Old-Fashioned,
Plain Jane, or
Oatmeal Chocolate
Chippers (page 10)
with

Buttercream
Frosting
(page 60)
or

Chocolate
Ganache
(page 64)

When all the sandwich cookies have their annual cookie convention, this one becomes everyone's secret crush. The oaties' good looks do make the heart beat faster. To make oatmeal creamwich cookies, you can either use a Plain Jane oatmeal cookie (no raisins, no chips, plain and proud) or one with raisins or chocolate chips.

Use a butter knife or small offset spatula to spread frosting or ganache on the underside of a cookie (or use a piping bag). Top with a second cookie to make a sandwich.

TREATS ARE GOOD! TREATS ARE GOOD! TREATS ARE GOOD! TREATS ARE GOOD! TREATS ARE GOOD! TREATS ARE GOOD! TREATS ARE GOOD! TREATS ARE GOOD! TREATS ARE GOOD! TRE
RE GOOD! TREATS ARE GOOD! TREATS ARE GOOD! TREATS ARE GOOD! TREATS ARE GOOD! TREATS ARE GOOD! TREATS ARE GOOD! TREATS ARE GOOD! TREATS ARE GOOD! TREATS ARE GOOD! TREA
E GOOD! TREATS ARE GOOD! TREATS ARE GOOD! TREATS ARE GOOD! TREATS ARE GOOD! TREATS ARE GOOD! TREATS ARE GOOD! TREATS ARE GOOD! TREATS ARE GOOD! TREATS ARE GOOD! TREATS ARE GOOD

RASPBERRY RINGS

Mix&Match
Sugar Dot
Sugar Cookies
(page 6) with

Meringue wash
(page 76),
plain sanding
sugar (page 78),
and raspberry jam

These sparkly cookies have a lovely flavor/texture combination. Looks and substance and razzle-dazzle to boot.

1   Preheat the oven to 350°F and grease a baking sheet or line it with parchment paper.

2   Roll out the sugar cookie dough to ¼ inch thick or just under. With a medium-size round cookie cutter (ours is 2½ inches across), cut out an even number of cookies. Use a smaller cookie cutter (ours is 1½ inches across) to cut a second hole in half of the cookies. Use a spatula to gently place the cookies on the baking sheet. Bake for 10 to 14 minutes, or until just barely tinted and toasty. Let cool completely.

3   Prepare the meringue wash in a small bowl.

4   Brush the tops of the cookies with the cut out circles with meringue wash and sprinkle them with a bit of sanding sugar. Set them aside to dry. (Note: I like to hold the cookie over a bowl when I sprinkle the sanding sugar to catch the sugar that doesn't make it onto the cookie.)

5   To assemble the sandwiches, pick up each of the whole cookies and spread a thin layer of jam on the underside of the cookie. Place the cookies jam side up on a tray as you finish. Place one cutout cookie over each of the jam-covered cookies to make a sandwich.

On Valentine's Day,
we make big heart-shaped versions of the raspberry ring, using a big heart cookie cutter and a little heart cookie cutter for the cutout in the center. You can also use a circle-shaped cookie cutter for the cookies and a little heart cookie cutter for the cutout. They make quite the Valentine!

TREATS ARE GOOD!

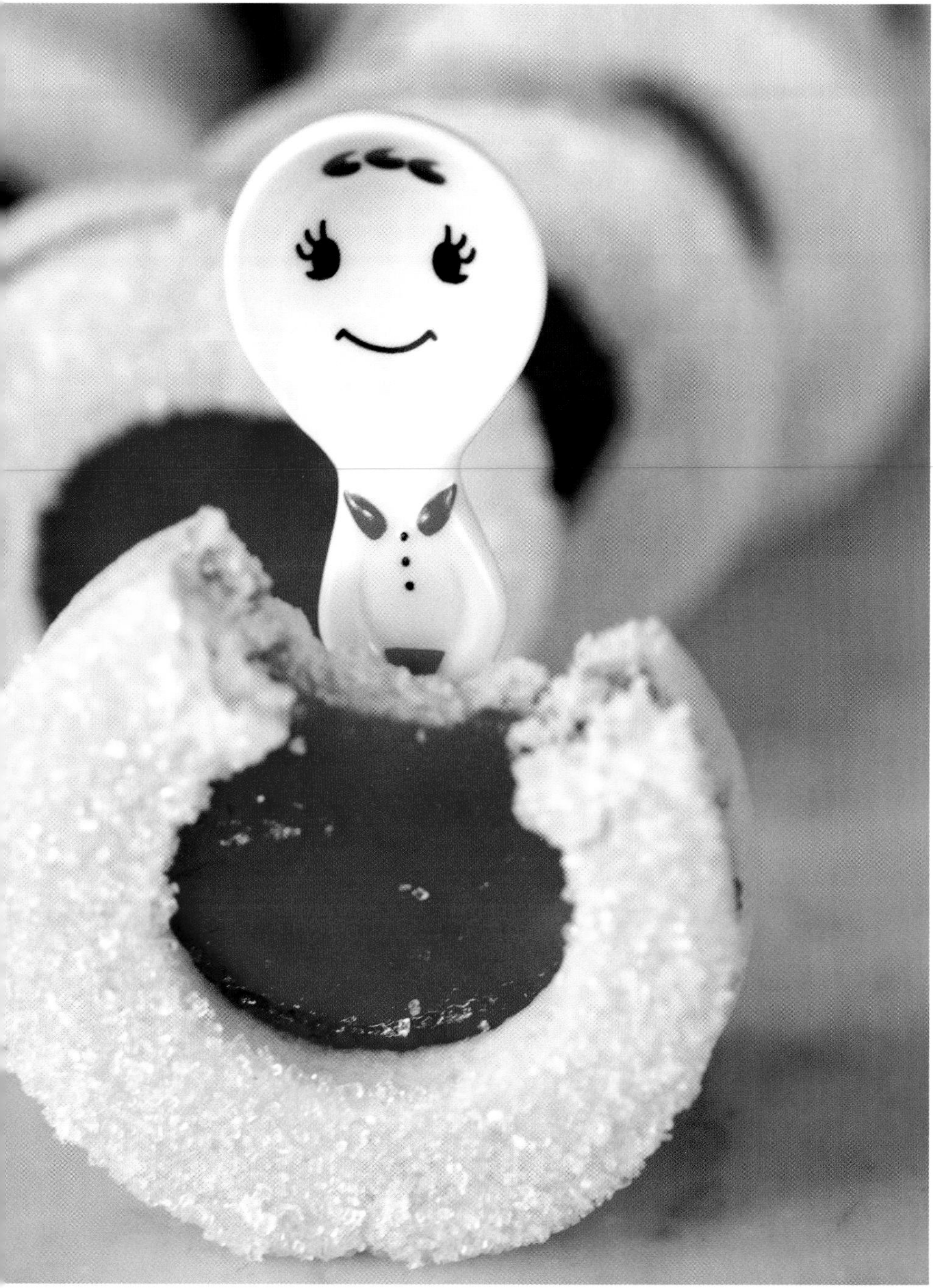

SUGAR & LEMON & APRICOT SANDWICH COOKIES

1 Preheat the oven to 350°F and grease a baking sheet or line it with parchment paper.

2 Roll out the sugar cookie dough to ¼ inch thick or just under. With a medium-size round cookie cutter (ours is 2½ inches across), cut out an even number of cookies. Use a spatula to gently place the cookies on the baking sheet. Bake for 10 to 14 minutes, or until just barely tinted and toasty. Let cool completely.

BUTTERCREAM SANDWICH COOKIES

Mix&Match
Sugar Dot
Sugar Cookies
(page 6) with

Buttercream Frosting
(page 60)

Spread a layer of buttercream frosting on the underside of a sugar cookie with a butter knife or pipe a dollop of frosting with a piping bag—your choice! Place a second cookie on top to make a sandwich. Use enough frosting so that when you press on the top layer, the frosting plumps out just enough to make you smile. If you like, you can roll the edges of the sandwich in sprinkles.

LEMON SANDWICH COOKIES

Mix&Match
Sugar Dot
Sugar Cookies
(page 6) with

Lemony Lemon Frosting
(page 62)

Follow the directions for the buttercream sandwich cookies, using lemony lemon frosting instead.

APRICOT SANDWICH COOKIES

Mix&Match
Sugar Dot
Sugar Cookies
(page 6) with

Apricot jam

Follow the directions for the buttercream sandwich cookies, using a thin layer of apricot jam. If you want to make apricot rings, see the Raspberry Rings recipe on page 30 and cut out the centers.

Note: You can leave the tops of the sandwiches plain, dust them with confectioners' sugar, or use meringue wash (page 76) and sanding sugar (page 78) for a sparkly top.

Today's Special Sandwich Cookie Is . . .

Chocolate cookies with peppermint frosting rolled in crushed peppermint candy!

Oatmeal cookies with raspberry jam and peanut butter filling!

Sugar cookies with espresso-flecked buttercream!

. . . Anything You Please!

Sugar cookies with strawberry jam and peanut butter filling!

Gingersnaps with caramel and almond bits!

Chocolate cookies with crushed malted milk balls, buttercream, and chocolate chips!

Delightful & Delicious!

A SANDWICH MADE WITH COOKIES.

I have a very special place in my heart for sandwich cookies. I love that they're just perfect for so many different occasions. Of course, any old day is a great time for a special sweet snack, but sometimes special days call for just the right touch! One man had us bake a super big chocolate Trucker the size of a cake for his wife's birthday. It really looked like a cookie made for a giant! And then sometimes we make little teeny tiny caramel creme sandwich cookies for filling little gift bags as party favors. And mini sandwich cookies are also perfect for an afternoon tea party for your favorite ten-year-olds and any doll guests who might just show up. From cake size to doll size, sandwich cookies are as delightful as they come!

(If you go a little crazy with all the sandwich possibilities, make a lot of sandwich cookies and throw a party just because…)

BROWNIES, BARS & SQUARES

Brownies are a crowd-pleasing, easy-to-bake treat that most of us grew up making at home.

They're great on the go, and so much fun to dress up. The best part of a brownie, in my opinion? Picking out just the right piece. Crispy or gooey? The one with lots of nuts or just a few? Which one is calling out your name?

And bars and squares! I love them. What's the difference between a bar and a square? Well . . . in a court of law, I'd have to admit, I think they're one and the same, but I like to use both names, as the fancy hits!

Brownies, bars, and squares are truly in a class of their own.

Not fancy. Supersatisfying.
And *soooo* good.

BROWNIES

The classic chocolate brownie is something I often crave and always love. Lots of kids and adults feel the same way, I am pretty well convinced. Think the smell of brownies baking will bring the neighbors over? Feel free to double the batch just in case!

Most everyone has a seriously impassioned opinion about what kind of brownie is the absolute best. Chewy! Cakey! Soft and gooey! But whatever your favorite style, when presented with a plate of homemade brownies, hardly anyone can resist having at least one (after all, it's only polite!). I offer you three great choices: a Chewy Brownie, a Cakey Brownie, and a Dark Chocolatey Brownie. Enjoy!

CHEWY BROWNIES

INGREDIENTS

¾ CUP (1½ STICKS) BUTTER

3 OUNCES UNSWEETENED CHOCOLATE

2 OUNCES DARK CHOCOLATE

1¼ CUPS SUGAR

2 EGGS

1½ TEASPOONS VANILLA EXTRACT

¾ CUP FLOUR

1 TABLESPOON COCOA POWDER

CAKEY BROWNIES

INGREDIENTS

¾ CUP (1½ STICKS) BUTTER

3 OUNCES UNSWEETENED CHOCOLATE

2 OUNCES DARK CHOCOLATE

1¼ CUPS SUGAR

3 EGGS

1½ TEASPOONS VANILLA EXTRACT

¾ CUP FLOUR

1 TABLESPOON COCOA POWDER

DARK CHOCOLATEY BROWNIES

INGREDIENTS

¾ CUP (1½ STICKS) BUTTER

1 OUNCE UNSWEETENED CHOCOLATE

5 OUNCES DARK CHOCOLATE

1 CUP SUGAR

2 EGGS

2 TEASPOONS VANILLA EXTRACT

⅔ CUP FLOUR

OPTIONAL FOR ALL BROWNIES!
½ cup semisweet chocolate chips
½ cup chopped pecans or walnuts

Makes 9 to 12 brownies

1. Preheat the oven to 350˚F and grease a 9 by 9-inch square pan (you can also line the pan with aluminum foil and grease the foil). Doubling the batch? Use a 9 by 13-inch pan.

2. Melt the butter and chocolates in a medium to large saucepan over low heat, or use a microwave. Watch carefully.

3. Meanwhile, gently beat the eggs in a bowl and stir in the vanilla.

4. When the butter and chocolate mixture is melted, take it off the heat and stir in the sugar, then the eggs and vanilla. Add the flour (and cocoa powder, if using) and stir well with a spoon or whisk, but do not overmix.

5. Pour the brownie batter into the prepared pan. (If you're using chocolate chips or nuts, mix them into the batter first and/or sprinkle them on top of the batter before baking, pressing them down a bit into the batter.)

6. Bake for 30 to 35 minutes, or until a knife or a toothpick inserted in the center comes out almost clean. Let the brownies cool before lifting them from the pan.

SPECIALS ARE GOOD! SPECIALS ARE GOOD! SPECIALS ARE GOOD! SPECIALS ARE GOOD! SPECIALS ARE GOOD! SPECIALS ARE GOOD! SPECIALS ARE GOOD! SPECIALS
GOOD! SPECIALS ARE GOOD! SPECIALS ARE GOOD! SPECIALS ARE GOOD! SPECIALS ARE GOOD! SPECIALS ARE GOOD! SPECIALS ARE GOOD! SPECIALS ARE GOOD! SPECIALS ARE GOOD!
OD! SPECIALS ARE GOOD! SPECIALS ARE GOOD! SPECIALS ARE GOOD! SPECIALS ARE GOOD! SPECIALS ARE GOOD! SPECIALS ARE GOOD! SPECIALS ARE GOOD! SPEC
PECIALS ARE GOOD! SPECIALS ARE GOOD! SPECIALS ARE GOOD! SPECIALS ARE GOOD! SPECIALS ARE GOOD! SPECIALS ARE GOOD! SPECIALS ARE GOOD! SPECIALS

BROWNIE SPECIALS

It's so easy to add a little something special to the top of a brownie. Bake a plain batch and then doll them up as you'd like! Since you're just adding an icing layer to the top of each brownie, you can make one special brownie or as many as you wish!

PEANUT BUTTER BROWNIES

Mix&Match Brownies (page 40) with

Chocolate Ganache Topping (page 64) & peanut butter

I like smooth peanut butter without added sugar best. Use your own favorite kind of peanut butter, of course!

Place the brownies on a plate or tray. With a butter knife or small offset spatula, spread warm chocolate toping on top of each brownie. (If the chocolate topping has been made earlier and stored in the fridge, warm it up in a microwave or in a double boiler.)

With a second knife, dollop some peanut butter on top of the chocolate-topped brownie. Swirl the peanut butter into the chocolate topping so that you blend them a bit, but don't fully mix it together. Repeat with each brownie.

CARAMEL BROWNIES

Mix&Match Brownies (page 40) with

Chocolate Ganache Topping (page 64) & Caramel Topping (page 70)

Place the brownies on a plate or tray. With a butter knife or small offset spatula, spread chocolate topping on top of each brownie. Drizzle caramel topping on top. Some of my bakers like to get fancy and make crisscross lines, curlicues, or squiggles. Sometimes I like to swoosh the caramel and chocolate together so that they're almost fully blended.

These guys are a little messier to make than the other special brownies, so the tray will definitely get schmutzy. Place your beautiful finished brownies on a clean plate or tray to serve!

ESPRESSO BROWNIES

Mix&Match Brownies (page 40) with

Chocolate Espresso Topping (page 65) & coffee beans

Place the brownies on a plate or tray. With a butter knife or small offset spatula, spread chocolate espresso topping on top of each brownie. Top with a few coffee beans. (You can toast the beans in the oven or toaster oven or use them as is.)

FEEL FREE TO EAT THE BROWNIES RIGHT AWAY, BUT LET THEM SET FOR A BIT OR CHILL A WHILE BEFORE PUTTING THEM IN A CONTAINER. THEY WILL KEEP WELL WRAPPED OR COVERED FOR 3 TO 5 DAYS IN A COOL, DRY SPOT OR IN THE FRIDGE.

RASPBERRY BROWNIES

1 BATCH BROWNIE BATTER (PAGE 40)

1 TO 1½ CUPS RASPBERRY JAM

These are a customer favorite! If you have a big crowd to please, you can double the recipe and use a bigger pan.

Makes 9 to 12 brownies

1   Preheat the oven to 350°F and grease a 9 by 9-inch pan (or a 9 by 13-inch pan for a double recipe).

2   Pour the brownie batter into the pan. Put the jam in a piping bag and pipe swirls of jam on top of the batter.

3   Bake for 35 to 40 minutes, or until a knife or toothpick comes out almost clean. (Adding the jam layer will add to the baking time. Every oven is a little different, so see how long you need.)

Note: Don't have a piping bag? Make one out of a sturdy plastic storage bag! Fill the bag partway, twist the top to keep the jam in place, and cut the tip of one corner of the bag. If you don't have a storage bag, drop dollops of jam on top of the brownie batter and swirl the jam into the batter a bit with a butter knife. It's best not to totally cover the top with jam.

TREATS ARE GOOD! TREATS ARE GOOD! TREATS ARE GOOD! TREATS ARE GOOD! TREATS ARE GOOD! TREATS ARE GOOD! TREATS ARE GOOD! TREATS ARE GOOD! TREATS ARE GOOD! TRE,
RE GOOD! TREATS ARE GOOD! TREATS ARE GOOD! TREATS ARE GOOD! TREATS ARE GOOD! TREATS ARE GOOD! TREATS ARE GOOD! TREATS ARE GOOD! TREATS ARE GOOD! TREATS ARE G
TREATS ARE GOOD! TREATS ARE GOOD! TREATS ARE GOOD! TREATS ARE GOOD! TREATS ARE GOOD! TREATS ARE GOOD! TREATS ARE GOOD! TREATS ARE GOOD! TREATS ARE GOOD! TREA
E GOOD! TREATS ARE GOOD! TREATS ARE GOOD! TREATS ARE GOOD! TREATS ARE GOOD! TREATS ARE GOOD! TREATS ARE GOOD! TREATS ARE GOOD! TREATS ARE GOOD! TREATS ARE GO

CREAM CHEESE BROWNIES

INGREDIENTS

1 BATCH BROWNIE BATTER (PAGE 40)

8 OUNCES CREAM CHEESE

⅓ CUP SUGAR

1 TEASPOON VANILLA EXTRACT

1 EGG

Add a cream cheese swirl to a brownie any time you'd like!

Makes 9 to 12 brownies

1 Preheat the oven to 350°F and grease a 9 by 9-inch pan.

2 Pour the brownie batter into the pan.

3 In a bowl or mixer, combine the cream cheese, sugar, vanilla, and egg. Mix well. Spread over the brownie batter. I recommend using a spoon or butter knife to make swirls of the cream cheese mixture in the brownie batter.

4 Bake for 35 to 40 minutes, or until a knife or toothpick comes out almost clean. (Adding the cream cheese layer will add to the baking time. Every oven is a little different, so see how long you need.)

EATS ARE GOOD! TREATS ARE GOOD! TREATS ARE GOOD! TREATS ARE GOOD! TREATS ARE GOOD! TREATS ARE GOOD! TREATS ARE GOOD! TREATS ARE GOOD! TREATS ARE GOOD! TREA
E GOOD! TREATS ARE GOOD! TREATS ARE GOOD! TREATS ARE GOOD! TREATS ARE GOOD! TREATS ARE GOOD! TREATS ARE GOOD! TREATS ARE GOOD! TREATS ARE GOOD! TREATS ARE GO
REATS ARE GOOD! TREATS ARE GOOD! TREATS ARE GOOD! TREATS ARE GOOD! TREATS ARE GOOD! TREATS ARE GOOD! TREATS ARE GOOD! TREATS ARE GOOD! TREATS ARE GOOD! TREA

Corner,

center,

or side?

What do you like best?

When customers order a brownie, I always ask, "Corner, center, or side?" If it's their first time at The Treats Truck, they often look surprised and say, "No one's ever asked me that before!" And with a big smile, they add, "A corner, please!"

Now, a corner is very different from a center, and while corners are quite nice, many swear by the center. Others prefer the side as the "best of both worlds." One of my favorite moments is when a couple comes to the truck and one person is surprised by the answer of the other. "A center? Really?" a husband asks his wife. "See," I say, "you think you know a person . . ."

The regulars throw the detail directly into their order. "Give me a center raspberry brownie and a corner pecan butterscotch." (The corners on that one are especially chewy and delicious, I must admit.)

MEXICAN CHOCOLATE BROWNIES

1 CUP (2 STICKS)
BUTTER

3 OUNCES
UNSWEETENED
CHOCOLATE

3 TABLETS MEXICAN
CHOCOLATE AND
½ TABLET, CHOPPED,
FOR THE TOPPING
(EACH TABLET IS
3.15 OUNCES)

1¾ CUPS PACKED
BROWN SUGAR

4 EGGS

2 TEASPOONS
VANILLA EXTRACT

1 TEASPOON
GROUND CINNAMON

1 CUP FLOUR

½ CUP MILK
CHOCOLATE OR
SEMISWEET
CHOCOLATE CHIPS
OR CHOPPED
CHOCOLATE

I love Mexican hot chocolate. I grew up drinking it and then fell in love with using the chocolate to make brownies. It has a wonderful combination of cinnamon, chocolate, and vanilla. You can get Mexican chocolate in some grocery stores or specialty stores, or you can order it by mail. I use mainly Ibarra or Abuelita because they're the most readily available.

Makes 9 to 12 brownies

1   Preheat the oven to 350°F and grease a 9 by 9-inch pan.

2   In a medium to large saucepan over low heat, melt the butter, unsweetened chocolate, and 3 tablets Mexican chocolate. Add the brown sugar and take off the heat.

3   Add the eggs and vanilla and stir. Add the cinnamon and flour and mix well. Pour the batter into the pan. Sprinkle the chopped Mexican chocolate and chocolate chips or chopped chocolate on top.

4   Bake for 30 to 35 minutes, or until a knife or toothpick comes out almost clean.

PECAN BUTTERSCOTCH BARS

INGREDIENTS

¾ CUP (1½ STICKS) BUTTER

2 CUPS DARK BROWN SUGAR

1½ CUPS FLOUR

1 TEASPOON SALT

2 TEASPOONS BAKING POWDER

2 EGGS

2 TEASPOONS VANILLA EXTRACT

1 CUP CHOPPED PECANS (OR WALNUTS)

This recipe is adapted from my friend's family's favorite recipe for butterscotch brownies. It's a superstar on The Treats Truck! Just one taste from the sample tray and you're hooked. If you don't like nuts, the bars are great without them, too.

Makes 9 to 12 bars

1   Preheat the oven to 350°F and grease a 9 by 9-inch pan (or double the recipe and use a 9 by 13-inch pan).

2   In a small saucepan over low heat, melt the butter. Add the brown sugar and stir.

3   In a medium bowl, mix the flour, salt, and baking powder.

4   Pour the butter-sugar mixture into the flour mixture and stir until combined. Add the egg and vanilla and stir well. Add ½ cup of the nuts and stir.

5   Pour the batter into the pan. Sprinkle the remaining nuts on top and pat them into place.

6   Bake for 25 to 30 minutes. They may look underdone, but they'll be chewily delicious when cool.

TREATS ARE GOOD! TREATS ARE GOOD!

SUPER-DUPER LAYER BARS

INGREDIENTS

½ CUP (1 STICK) BUTTER, MELTED

1½ CUPS GRAHAM CRACKER CRUMBS (SEE NOTE)

1 CUP SEMISWEET OR MILK CHOCOLATE CHIPS

1 CUP BUTTERSCOTCH CHIPS, PEANUT BUTTER CHIPS, WHITE CHOCOLATE CHIPS, AND OTHER ADD-INS, SUCH AS TOFFEE CHIPS, DRIED CHERRIES, OR CHOPPED DRIED APRICOTS (USE 2 OR 3 CUPS IN ALL!)

1 CUP CHOPPED NUTS (ANY KIND YOU PLEASE!)

1½ CUPS SHREDDED SWEETENED COCONUT

ONE 14-OUNCE CAN SWEETENED CONDENSED MILK

These are often called seven-layer bars, but I like to call them Super-Dupers, because they're so delicious and easy to make. You can layer in so many tasty bits and pieces!

Makes 9 to 12 bars

1   Preheat the oven to 350°F and grease a 9 by 9-inch pan (double the recipe and use a 9 by 13-inch pan if you want a big batch).

2   Melt the butter in a saucepan over low heat or the microwave. Mix the melted butter with the graham cracker crumbs and press the crust mixture down to cover the bottom of the pan (or you can melt the butter in the pan itself and press the crumbs into place on top of the melted butter).

3   Layer each of your chosen ingredients except one on top of the graham cracker crust. Pour the condensed milk on top of the ingredients (it doesn't need to be a solid layer), then sprinkle the top with your last ingredient.

4   Bake for 25 minutes. Let cool before cutting.

Note: For a gluten-free option, just leave out the graham cracker crumbs and butter! Instead, use 1½ to 2 cups chocolate chips mixed with ¾ cup coconut as the first layer.

TREATS ARE GOOD! TREATS ARE GOOD!

THE CLASSIC RICE CRISPY SQUARE

INGREDIENTS

3 TABLESPOONS BUTTER, PLUS 1 MORE TO GREASE THE PAN

10 OUNCES MINI-MARSHMALLOWS (THE REGULAR SIZE IS FINE, TOO)

6 CUPS CRISPY RICE CEREAL

Note: If you don't have a big pot, melt the marshmallows and butter in a smaller pot or saucepan. Pour the cereal in a bowl big enough for the whole mix, then pour the marshmallow mixture into the bowl.

We serve a lot of rice crispy squares at The Treats Truck every day, and we also cater a lot of parties, including weddings. We often fill boxes of treats for the guests to take home at the end of the party. No matter how fancy the event or how elegant the guests, one of the most popular items is . . . the classic rice crispy square. As kids, a lot of us made them at home or in the Girl Scouts (that's how I earned my cooking badge). The combination of marshmallow and butter with the crispy rice cereal . . . there's just something about it!

Makes one giant crispy (okay, okay, or many pieces if you insist on sharing)

1   Use 1 tablespoon of the butter to grease an 8 by 8-inch, 9 by 9-inch, or 9 by 13-inch pan, depending on how thick you want your treats (you can also halve or double the recipe).

2   Melt the 3 tablespoons butter in a big pot over low heat. When the butter has melted enough to coat the bottom of the pot, add the marshmallows. Stir often until melted, then remove from the heat.

3   Pour the rice cereal into the pot and stir until the marshmallows and cereal are mixed together.

4   Use a bowl scraper or spatula to get all the mixture out of the pot and into the pan. Pat into place without pressing down too hard. Butter is your friend here—butter your hands if it helps!

5   Let the crispy squares set for at least 15 minutes before cutting. Store them in plastic wrap or an airtight container for up to 2 days. The fresher the better, so eating them the same day you make them is best.

Crispies!

the KITCHEN SINK

the CLASSIC

the CRAN-ALMOND

CRAN-ALMOND CRISPY SQUARES

INGREDIENTS

3 TABLESPOONS BUTTER, PLUS 1 MORE TO GREASE THE PAN

5 CUPS CRISPY RICE CEREAL

1 CUP CRISPY WHOLE WHEAT CEREAL, SUCH AS UNCLE SAM

½ CUP DRIED CRANBERRIES

½ CUP WHOLE ALMONDS

ONE 10-OUNCE BAG MINI-MARSHMALLOWS (BIG MARSHMALLOWS ARE OKAY, TOO)

I'm a big fan of this one. The mix of almonds, dried cranberries, and cereal tastes great, and, of course, the marshmallows and butter help make the magic happen.

Makes 9 to 12 squares

1 Grease a 9 by 9-inch pan with 1 tablespoon of the butter.

2 In a big bowl, combine the cereals, cranberries, and almonds. Set aside.

3 Melt the 3 tablespoons butter in a big pot over low heat. When the butter has melted enough to coat the bottom of the pot, add the marshmallows. Stir often until melted, then remove from the heat.

4 Pour the cereal mixture into the butter-marshmallow mixture. Mix well!

5 Use a bowl scraper or spatula to get all the crispy goodness out of the pot and into the pan. Pat into place without pressing down too hard. Butter is your friend here—butter your hands if it helps!

6 Let the crispy squares stand for at least 15 minutes to set before cutting into bars.

7 Store the crispy squares in plastic wrap or an airtight container. Keep them in a cool, dry place in your kitchen. They are best when superfresh but will last a few days.

Note: If you don't have a big pot, melt the marshmallows and butter in a smaller pot or saucepan, then pour the marshmallow mixture into the bowl of cereal and cranberries.

KITCHEN SINK CRISPY SQUARES

INGREDIENTS

3 TABLESPOONS BUTTER, PLUS 1 MORE TO GREASE THE PAN

ONE 10-OUNCE BAG MINI-MARSHMALLOWS

⅓ CUP PEANUT BUTTER

5½ TO 6 CUPS CRISPY RICE CEREAL

1 HANDFUL BROKEN THIN PRETZEL STICKS

1 SMALL PACK M&M CANDIES

1 HANDFUL CHOCOLATE CHIPS

¼ CUP CONFETTI SPRINKLES, OPTIONAL BUT ENCOURAGED

I love the name "Kitchen Sink" and the invitation it gives you to throw crazy combinations of ingredients together. Plan ahead and get all your favorite add-ins at the grocery store, or if you want, just open your cupboard and see what possibilities appear inside! Coconut, candy, pretzels, breakfast cereals—what will you find?

Here's our most popular Kitchen Sink recipe. Feel free to adapt as you wish.

Makes 9 to 12 squares

1   Grease a 9 by 9-inch pan with 1 tablespoon of the butter.

2   Melt the 3 tablespoons of butter in a big pot over low heat. Add the marshmallows and stir often until they are fully melted. Add the peanut butter and mix until melted.

3   Pour the cereal into the pot of marshmallow mixture and mix well, adding in the pretzels, M&Ms, and chocolate chips as you stir. While you're at it, throw in the sprinkles, if you have some handy! Use a pan scraper or silicone spatula to move the mixture into the pan.

4   Let stand for at least 15 minutes to set before cutting into bars.

Note: If you don't have a big pot, melt the marshmallows and butter in a smaller pot or saucepan. Pour the cereal and add-ins into a bowl big enough for the whole mix, then pour the marshmallow mixture into the bowl.

TIP: EXPECTING A BIG CROWD?
Just double the recipe, or make a couple of small batches and vary the add-ins for each batch just for fun.

APRICOT SQUARES

This is a really yummy bar we feature as a Special at Passover time. Lots of people like the bar, whether they celebrate Passover or not—the apricot jam with fresh lemon juice is delicious!

BAR LAYER

1 CUP (2 STICKS) BUTTER

2 EGG YOLKS

1 DASH SALT

1 CUP SUGAR

2 CUPS MATZO CAKE MEAL (OR GROUND MATZO; SEE NOTE)

2 TEASPOONS LEMON ZEST

1 TEASPOON VANILLA EXTRACT

JAM LAYER

1 CUP APRICOT JAM

¼ CUP FRESHLY SQUEEZED LEMON JUICE

Makes 9 to 12 squares

1   Preheat the oven to 350°F.

2   To make the bar layer, cream the butter with a mixer. With the mixer going, add the egg yolks, then the salt, sugar, matzo cake meal, lemon zest, and vanilla.

3   Pour the mixture into a 9 by 9-inch pan and press to cover the bottom of the pan. Try to make a slightly higher ridge at the edges.

4   Bake for 20 to 25 minutes. Set aside to cool.

5   To prepare the jam layer, combine the jam and lemon juice. Pour the jam mixture into the pan and spread it evenly over the crust, staying away from the edges.

6   Bake for 20 to 25 minutes more. Cool completely before cutting. Store, wrapped or in a covered container, for 3 to 5 days.

*Note: **If you can't find matzo cake meal, you can make your own by putting plain matzo in the blender or food processor.***

LEMON SQUARES

A classic—so lemony, buttery good!

CRUST

2 CUPS FLOUR

½ CUP CONFECTIONERS' SUGAR

1 CUP (2 STICKS) COLD BUTTER

PINCH SALT

LEMON LAYER

4 EGGS

2 CUPS WHITE SUGAR

1 TEASPOON BAKING POWDER

½ CUP FRESHLY SQUEEZED LEMON JUICE

1 TABLESPOON LEMON ZEST

CONFECTIONERS' SUGAR, FOR DUSTING THE TOP

Makes 9 to 12 squares

1   Line a 9 by 9-inch pan with aluminum foil.

2   In a medium bowl, combine the flour and confectioners' sugar. Cut in the butter until you have a fine crumbly mixture. Press into the pan.

3   Bake for 20 to 25 minutes, or until golden.

4   While the bottom layer is baking, prepare the lemon mixture. In a medium bowl, whisk together all the ingredients.

5   Pour the lemon mixture over the baked crust as soon as it comes out of the oven. Bake for 20 to 25 minutes.

6   Cool before cutting. The bars will last for 3 to 5 days wrapped and kept cool or refrigerated.

FROSTINGS, FILLINGS & TOPPINGS, SPRINKLES & SUGAR

I get pretty excited when it's time to frost a cake or put the finishing touches on a cookie. Putting it all together is so satisfying. There's something so pleasurable in the anticipation of serving what you've baked.

TIP: MOST FROSTINGS, FILLINGS, AND TOPPINGS CAN EASILY BE MADE AHEAD OF TIME TO SAVE TIME LATER.

TIP: About 4 cups of frosting is a good amount for a two-layer 9-inch cake or a batch of 24 cupcakes, but you can also make a larger batch when you want an extra-generous amount of frosting at the ready!

Besides being superdelicious, frostings, fillings, and toppings are your go-to magic kit for dressing up cookies, sandwich cookies, brownies, and cakes. Mix and match to your heart's desire! You're sure to win oohs and aahs and blissful mmmms from all your friends and family.

And be sure to use sprinkles. What can I say? Sprinkles make me smile.

Adding sprinkles or sparkly sanding sugar to a cookie or a cupcake makes people happy. Customers often point to the very cookie they want. *The one over there with lots of sprinkles* or *That orange flower cookie with the pink center, please!* I especially love when adults in business attire get as excited as the kids about picking out just the right one. The delight factor is one of the things I love best about treats!

BUTTERCREAM FROSTING

INGREDIENTS

½ CUP (1 STICK)
BUTTER, SOFTENED

6 CUPS SIFTED
CONFECTIONERS'
SUGAR

½ CUP WHOLE MILK

1½ TEASPOONS
VANILLA EXTRACT

I love cupcakes topped with buttercream frosting and sprinkles, buttercream-frosted devil's food cake, and buttercream iced sugar cookies. In addition to its old-fashioned charms, buttercream can be a blank canvas—you can tint it any color, and depending on how you're using it, you can add more milk or sugar to get the consistency you want—not too thick, not too thin—just the way you want it. I also use the basic buttercream as a base for making different kinds of frostings, like chocolate or coconut.

A small batch of buttercream is good for most cookie batches or 2 dozen cupcakes, or a frosted double-layer cake (or make 1½ batches if you want a little reserve for good measure). Make a double batch for a big batch of treats or for making more than one kind of frosting.

Makes 4 cups

1   In a bowl or mixer, cream the butter. Add the confectioners' sugar 2 cups at a time, mixing well as you go. Add the milk and vanilla and mix until smooth and creamy.

2   Stick the frosting in the fridge for 20 to 30 minutes to firm up before using. If you make it ahead of time to use another day, take it out of the fridge with enough time for it to sit on the counter to soften, or stick it in the microwave for a short zap. The frosting keeps for up to 2 weeks.

It's always a good idea to sift the confectioners' sugar first to get out any little lumps. If you don't have a sifter or strainer, pour the sugar into a bowl and mash it with a fork.

CHOCOLATE FROSTING

INGREDIENTS

8 OUNCES
UNSWEETENED
CHOCOLATE

¼ CUP PLUS
2 TABLESPOONS
HEAVY CREAM

4 CUPS
BUTTERCREAM
FROSTING
(PAGE 60)

Chocolate. Yum. This is one of the frostings I use the most. Both vanilla and chocolate frosting add the perfect top to cakes and cupcakes!

Makes about 4 cups

1   Melt the chocolate in a double boiler or saucepan, then stir in the cream. (You can also melt the chocolate carefully in a microwave oven, putting it in for just 15 to 30 seconds at a time.)

2   Put the batch of softened buttercream frosting in a bowl or mixer (take it out of the fridge with enough time for it to sit on the counter to soften, or stick it in the microwave for a short zap).

3   Mix the buttercream in the bowl, adding in the chocolate mixture. Mix together until smooth and combined.

*Note: **For a darker chocolate frosting, add 2 to 3 ounces dark chocolate to the melted chocolate and cream.***

Mix&Match
Chocolate Frosting and Buttercream Frosting with cakes & cupcakes!

LEMONY LEMON FROSTING

This lemon frosting is great for cakes or sugar cookies. We use it on top of sugar cookies to make lemony lemon dot cookies! For cakes, we make a supercreamy version of the frosting, while for cookies, we prefer an icier lemon frosting. Here are the recipes for both!

INGREDIENTS

1 CUP (2 STICKS) BUTTER, SOFTENED

6 CUPS SIFTED CONFECTIONERS' SUGAR

2 TABLESPOONS LEMON ZEST

½ CUP FRESHLY SQUEEZED LEMON JUICE

FOR CAKES

Makes 4 cups

1   In a bowl or standing mixer cream the butter, slowly. Add the confectioners' sugar and mix well. Add the lemon zest and lemon juice. Mix until smooth and creamy.

2   Keep in a covered container in the refrigerator for up to 2 weeks.

Mix&Match with Our Favorite Vanilla Cake (page 84)

INGREDIENTS

½ CUP (1 STICK) BUTTER

4 CUPS SIFTED CONFECTIONERS' SUGAR

1 TABLESPOON LEMON ZEST

3 TO 4 TABLESPOONS FRESHLY SQUEEZED LEMON JUICE

FOR COOKIES

Makes 1¼ cups

1   Melt the butter in a medium saucepan over low heat.

2   In a big bowl or mixer, combine the confectioners' sugar and butter and stir well. Add the lemon zest and lemon juice. Add more lemon juice if the icing seems too thick.

3   Keep in a covered container in the refrigerator for up to 2 weeks.

Mix&Match with Sugar Dot Sugar Cookies (page 6) for Lemony Lemon Dot Cookies (page 7) and Lemon Sandwich Cookies (page 32)

TREATS ARE GOOD! TREATS ARE GOOD! TREATS ARE GOOD! TREATS ARE GOOD! TREATS ARE GOOD! TREATS ARE GOOD! TREATS ARE GOOD! TREATS ARE GOOD! TREATS ARE GOOD! TRE
RE GOOD! TREATS ARE GOOD! TREATS ARE GOOD! TREATS ARE GOOD! TREATS ARE GOOD! TREATS ARE GOOD! TREATS ARE GOOD! TREATS ARE GOOD! TREATS ARE GOOD! TREATS ARE G
TEATS ARE GOOD! TREATS ARE GOOD! TREATS ARE GOOD! TREATS ARE GOOD! TREATS ARE GOOD! TREATS ARE GOOD! TREATS ARE GOOD! TREATS ARE GOOD! TREATS ARE GOOD! TREATS ARE
GOOD! TREATS ARE GOOD! TREATS ARE GOOD! TREATS ARE GOOD! TREATS ARE GOOD! TREATS ARE GOOD! TREATS ARE GOOD! TREATS ARE GOOD! TREATS ARE GOOD! TREATS ARE GOOD! TRE

CREAM CHEESE FROSTING

INGREDIENTS

¾ CUP (1 ½ STICKS)
BUTTER, SOFTENED

12 OUNCES CREAM
CHEESE, SOFTENED

3 CUPS SIFTED
CONFECTIONERS'
SUGAR

2 TEASPOONS
VANILLA EXTRACT

This frosting is so delicious on carrot or pumpkin cake. I like to put a nice thick layer on top of our cakes. Sometimes, a customer will ask if we have even more frosting in the back. An extra dollop? I look both ways to make sure no one's looking, and then—magically—extra frosting might just find its way onto their slice of cake.

Makes about 5 cups

In a bowl or mixer, cream the butter. Add the cream cheese. Cream until fully combined. Add the confectioners' sugar and vanilla and beat until smooth. Keep refrigerated and covered until ready to use. This frosting can be made ahead of time and keeps well for over a week.

Mix&Match with Pumpkin Cake (page 103), Carrot Cake (page 87), or Banana Cake (page 88)

LEMONY CREAM CHEESE FROSTING

The right cake paired with this lemony cream cheese frosting makes for one delicious duo.

Mix 3 to 5 tablespoons freshly squeezed lemon juice and 2 tablespoons lemon zest into cream cheese frosting.

Mix&Match with Our Favorite Vanilla Cake (page 84), Poppy Seed Cake (page 93), Lemon Cake (page 90), or Coconut Cake (page 92)

CHOCOLATE GANACHE: FROSTING, FILLING & TOPPING

INGREDIENTS

2 CUPS SEMISWEET CHOCOLATE (CHIPS OR CHOPPED CHOCOLATE)

¾ TO 1 CUP HEAVY CREAM

Chocolate ganache is basically a mixture of chocolate and cream—thick, velvety, and oh so good. I just call it a baker's best friend! It's so versatile. As a frosting, filling, and topping, it's great for sandwich cookies and cakes and on top of brownies. Start with a good chocolate you really like. I often use Callebaut chocolate, but there are so many wonderful ones out there to try!

Makes about 2 cups

All you do is melt the chocolate and heavy cream together! As you go, your ganache can easily be made a little thicker or thinner as needed, by adding a bit more chocolate or a bit more cream.

YOU CAN MAKE CHOCOLATE GANACHE A COUPLE OF DIFFERENT WAYS:

Use a double boiler or saucepan. Be sure to watch carefully and stir often.

Use the microwave. Zap the chocolate and cream for just 30 seconds, then give it a good stir to help melt the chocolate. As many times as needed, stick it in again for 15 to 20 seconds at a time.

FOR A FROSTING, let the ganache cool. You can use a whisk to whip it up before using it as a frosting or use the cooled ganache as is. For a filling or topping, no need to cool or whip. You can use it immediately or keep it in the fridge and warm it up when you're ready. The ganache can be kept in the fridge for 2 weeks or more.

CHOCOLATE ESPRESSO FILLING & TOPPING

This is so good and easy. Adding instant espresso powder to your chocolate ganache makes a great filling or topping for cookies and brownies. You can find espresso powder at the grocery store and keep it in your cupboard for whenever the mood strikes you. If you can't find instant espresso powder, use regular instant coffee instead. All you do is mix a bit of instant espresso powder (start with 1 teaspoon) into the chocolate ganache, stir, and add more a teaspoon at a time to suit your taste.

MINT CHOCOLATE FILLING & TOPPING

Add a nice chopped mint chocolate bar or even Junior Mints or other mint chocolate candy when you're melting the chocolate for your ganache. I like 1 part mint chocolate to 2 parts semisweet chocolate, but you can change the balance as you please!

PEPPERMINT FROSTING

1 CUP BUTTERCREAM FROSTING (PAGE 60)

2 TO 3 TABLESPOONS FINELY CRUSHED CANDY CANES OR OTHER PEPPERMINT CANDY

I love using crushed candy canes in frosting or as sprinkles on cookies. Especially around Christmastime, peppermint candy is such a fun addition to all kinds of treats! Each December, we bake candy cane–shaped sugar cookies and frost them with this frosting, and top both chocolate and vanilla cupcakes with it as well.

Makes 1 cup

Mix the frosting and candy well. Give it another quick mix just before using.

Mix&Match with

Sugar Dot Sugar Cookies (page 6),

Chocolate Cookies (page 12), or

Cupcakes (page 95)

TIP: IT'S EVEN BETTER IF YOU REFRIGERATE IT OVERNIGHT— IT GETS SO PEPPERMINTY GOOD!

TREATS ARE GOOD! TREATS ARE GOOD! TREATS ARE GOOD! TREATS ARE GOOD! TREATS ARE GOOD! TREATS ARE GOOD! TREATS ARE GOOD! TREATS ARE GOOD! TREATS ARE GOOD! TR
RE GOOD! TREATS ARE GOOD! TREATS ARE GOOD! TREATS ARE GOOD! TREATS ARE GOOD! TREATS ARE GOOD! TREATS ARE GOOD! TREATS ARE GOOD! TREATS ARE GOOD! TREATS ARE G
TREATS ARE GOOD! TREATS ARE GOOD! TREATS ARE GOOD! TREATS ARE GOOD! TREATS ARE GOOD! TREATS ARE GOOD! TREATS ARE GOOD! TREATS ARE GOOD! TREATS ARE GOOD! TREA
RE GOOD! TREATS ARE GOOD! TREATS ARE GOOD! TREATS ARE GOOD! TREATS ARE GOOD! TREATS ARE GOOD! TREATS ARE GOOD! TREATS ARE GOOD! TREATS ARE GOOD! TREATS ARE G

CANDY FROSTING

INGREDIENTS

1 TO 3 TABLESPOONS FINELY CRUSHED OR CHOPPED CANDY OF YOUR CHOICE

1 CUP BUTTERCREAM FROSTING (PAGE 60) OR CHOCOLATE FROSTING (PAGE 61)

The inspiration for candy frosting came from an ice cream store nearby that used to make a wonderful crushed candy ice cream. I loved seeing what they decided to add each week to the mix! Use your favorite candy, like chocolate bars, toffee, old-fashioned candy sticks, Snickers, Twix bars, or Red Hots, to name a few.

Makes 1 cup

Finely chop or crush the candy. If crushing hard candy, put it in a sturdy plastic bag or wrap very well in plastic wrap. Use a good smasher (the back of an ice cream scoop, a meat tenderizing mallet, or some other creative solution) to pound the candy until it's candy dust and teeny bits. Mix the frosting in a container or bowl with the finely chopped/crushed candy. Voilà!

Mix&Match with

Cupcakes
(page 95)

COCONUT FROSTING

**1 CUP SHREDDED
SWEETENED
COCONUT**

**2 CUPS
BUTTERCREAM
FROSTING (PAGE 60)**

While there are recipes to make coconut frosting from scratch, I prefer this simple method using our buttercream frosting. Mix and match with your favorite cakes and cupcakes! For a cake or a large batch of cupcakes, make a double recipe.

Makes 2 cups

Thoroughly mix the coconut and frosting. Add more coconut as a garnish on top of your desserts as needed.

Mix&Match with Coconut Cake (page 92) or Lemon Cake (page 90)

CINNAMON FROSTING

INGREDIENTS

**1 TO 2 TEASPOONS
GROUD CINNAMON**

**1 CUP BUTTERCREAM
FROSTING (PAGE 60)**

Add a teaspoon or two of cinnamon to buttercream frosting for a quick cinnamon frosting!

Makes 1 cup

Just dust your buttercream frosting with some cinnamon and mix well. Nice and easy and cinnamony good.

Mix&Match with Cinnamon Cookies (page 15) or Cinnamon Sandwich Cookies (page 25)

TREATS ARE GOOD! TREATS ARE GOOD! TREATS ARE GOOD! TREATS ARE GOOD! TREATS ARE GOOD! TREATS ARE GOOD! TREATS ARE GOOD! TREATS ARE GOOD! TREATS ARE GOOD! TRE.
RE GOOD! TREATS ARE GOOD! TREATS ARE GOOD! TREATS ARE GOOD! TREATS ARE GOOD! TREATS ARE GOOD! TREATS ARE GOOD! TREATS ARE GOOD! TREATS ARE G
TREATS ARE GOOD! TREATS ARE GOOD! TREATS ARE GOOD! TREATS ARE GOOD! TREATS ARE GOOD! TREATS ARE GOOD! TREATS ARE GOOD! TREATS ARE GOOD! TREA
E GOOD! TREATS ARE GOOD! TREATS ARE GOOD! TREATS ARE GOOD! TREATS ARE GOOD! TREATS ARE GOOD! TREATS ARE GOOD! TREATS ARE GOOD! TREATS ARE GOOD! TREATS A

PEANUT BUTTER FILLING

INGREDIENTS

½ TO 1 CUP DARK
BROWN SUGAR

1 CUP SMOOTH
PEANUT BUTTER
(NO SUGAR ADDED)

This is the filling we use for our peanut butter sandwich cookies and peanut butter Truckers. I find the combination of peanut butter and dark brown sugar just right in terms of flavor and texture. I like to use a smooth peanut butter without any added sugar.

Makes about 1¼ cups

Put the brown sugar in a bowl and mash it with a fork to remove any lumps. Add the peanut butter and mix well with a sturdy spoon or your hands (I know! But just try it, you might like it!). Store in a covered container in the fridge until ready to use. This filling keeps very well and can be used over a few weeks.

Note: Equal parts peanut butter and sugar is great, and so is 1 part sugar to 2 parts peanut butter. See which you like best!

Mix&Match with
Peanut Butter
Cookies (page 5) to
make Peanut Butter
Sandwich Cookies
(page 28)

Chocolate Cookies
(page 12) to make
Peanut Butter
Chocolate Truckers
(page 27)

REATS ARE GOOD! TREATS ARE GOOD! TREATS ARE GOOD! TREATS ARE GOOD! TREATS ARE GOOD! TREATS ARE GOOD! TREATS ARE GOOD! TREATS ARE GOOD! TREATS ARE GOOD! TREAT
TREATS ARE GOOD! TREATS ARE GOOD! TREATS ARE GOOD! TREATS ARE GOOD! TREATS ARE GOOD! TREATS ARE GOOD! TREATS ARE GOOD! TREATS ARE GOOD! TREATS ARE GOOD! TREATS AR
TREATS ARE GOOD! TREATS ARE GOOD! TREATS ARE GOOD! TREATS ARE GOOD! TREATS ARE GOOD! TREATS ARE GOOD! TREATS ARE GOOD! TREATS ARE GOOD! TREATS ARE GOOD! TREATS AR

TREATS ARE GOOD! TREATS ARE GOOD! TREATS ARE GOOD! TREATS ARE GOOD! TREATS ARE GOOD! TREATS ARE GOOD! TREATS ARE GOOD! TREATS ARE GOOD! TREATS ARE GOOD! TRE
TREATS ARE GOOD! TREATS ARE GOOD! TREATS ARE GOOD! TREATS ARE GOOD! TREATS ARE GOOD! TREATS ARE GOOD! TREATS ARE GOOD! TREATS ARE GOOD! TREATS ARE GOOD! TRE
TREATS ARE GOOD! TREATS ARE GOOD! TREATS ARE GOOD! TREATS ARE GOOD! TREATS ARE GOOD! TREATS ARE GOOD! TREATS ARE GOOD! TREATS ARE GOOD! TREATS ARE GOOD! TRE
TREATS ARE GOOD! TREATS ARE GOOD! TREATS ARE GOOD! TREATS ARE GOOD! TREATS ARE GOOD! TREATS ARE GOOD! TREATS ARE GOOD! TREATS ARE GOOD! TREATS ARE GC

CARAMEL TOPPING

INGREDIENTS

CARAMEL CANDIES (SUCH AS KRAFT)

HEAVY CREAM

We use a caramel topping on brownies and brownie sundaes, and sometimes on cakes. I like to use the small cube-shaped caramels you can buy in a bag at the grocery store. It is easy to keep a bag of caramel squares in your pantry for whenever the mood strikes you. Generally, for topping on brownies, it can be thicker, and for sundaes and cakes, it should be thinner.

Make as little or as much as you need

All you do is melt the caramels with the heavy cream. Start with a small amount of cream with the caramel and add more as needed to make the topping thicker or thinner.

THERE ARE TWO WAYS TO DO IT:

Use a double boiler or saucepan. Be sure to watch carefully and stir often.

OR

Use the microwave. Zap the caramels and cream for just 30 seconds, then give it a good stir to help melt the caramel. As needed, stick it back in again for just 15 to 20 seconds at a time.

Mix&Match with

Brownie Sundaes (page 139),

Caramel Brownies (page 43), or

Dessert Nachos (page 136)

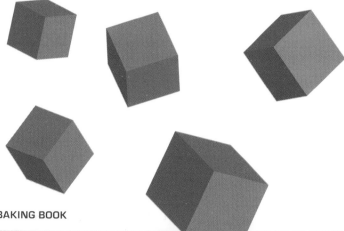

TREATS ARE GOOD! TREATS ARE GOOD! TREATS ARE GOOD! TREATS ARE GOOD! TREATS ARE GOOD! TREATS ARE GOOD! TREATS ARE GOOD! TREATS ARE GOOD! TREATS ARE GOOD! TREAT
TREATS ARE GOOD! TREATS ARE GOOD! TREATS ARE GOOD! TREATS ARE GOOD! TREATS ARE GOOD! TREATS ARE GOOD! TREATS ARE GOOD! TREATS ARE GOOD! TREATS ARE GOOD! TREAT
TREATS ARE GOOD! TREATS ARE GOOD! TREATS ARE GOOD! TREATS ARE GOOD! TREATS ARE GOOD! TREATS ARE GOOD! TREATS ARE GOOD! TREATS ARE GOOD! TREATS ARE GOOD! TREAT;

TREATS ARE GOOD! TREATS ARE GOOD! TREATS ARE GOOD! TREATS ARE GOOD! TREATS ARE GOOD! TREATS ARE GOOD! TREATS ARE GOOD! TREATS ARE GOOD! TREATS ARE GOOD! TRE
ARE GOOD! TREATS ARE GOOD! TREATS ARE GOOD! TREATS ARE GOOD! TREATS ARE GOOD! TREATS ARE GOOD! TREATS ARE GOOD! TREATS ARE GOOD! TREATS ARE GOOD! TREATS ARE G
TREATS ARE GOOD! TREATS ARE GOOD! TREATS ARE GOOD! TREATS ARE GOOD! TREATS ARE GOOD! TREATS ARE GOOD! TREATS ARE GOOD! TREATS ARE GOOD! TREATS ARE GOOD! TREA
E GOOD! TREATS ARE GOOD! TREATS ARE GOOD! TREATS ARE GOOD! TREATS ARE GOOD! TREATS ARE GOOD! TREATS ARE GOOD! TREATS ARE GOOD! TREATS ARE GOOD! TREATS ARE GG

HOT FUDGE TOPPING

INGREDIENTS

8 OUNCES DARK CHOCOLATE

7 TABLESPOONS BUTTER

½ CUP SUGAR

½ CUP HEAVY CREAM

¼ CUP HOT WATER

1 TEASPOON VANILLA EXTRACT

PINCH SALT

While store-bought hot fudge topping is good, homemade is even better!

Makes about 2 cups

Melt the chocolate and butter in a saucepan over low heat. Stir in the sugar, heavy cream, and hot water. Add the vanilla and salt. Use right away or set aside until ready to use. Just before using, warm the topping in the microwave or on the stove. Refrigerate any leftovers. It'll keep for a few weeks, that is, if it lasts that long!

Mix&Match with

Brownie Sundaes (page 139),

Ice Cream Pie (page 144),

Ice Cream Cake (page 145), or

Dessert Nachos (page 136)

GLAZES

On some kinds of cake, a glaze adds a wonderful icy zing and an added burst of flavor.

LEMON GLAZE

INGREDIENTS

Makes about ½ cup

1½ CUPS CONFECTIONERS' SUGAR

3½ TABLESPOONS FRESHLY SQUEEZED LEMON JUICE

You can add more sugar or lemon juice, as needed to make the glaze the right consistency. It should be liquidy enough to drizzle or pour over a cake.

Mix&Match with Poppy Seed Cake (page 93) or Lemon Cake (page 90)

CHOCOLATE GLAZE

INGREDIENTS

I like using just chocolate and cream, so it is a ganache glaze.

4 OUNCES SEMISWEET CHOCOLATE, CHOPPED

½ CUP HEAVY CREAM, WARMED

Makes ¾ cup

Add chocolate or heavy cream as needed to get the right consistency and the amount of glaze you want. Pour the glaze over your cake and give it time to set before serving.

Mix&Match with Poppy Seed Cake (page 93), Banana Cake (page 88), or Our Favorite Chocolate Cake (page 85)

COFFEE GLAZE

![INGREDIENTS]

Makes ½ cup

**1 TABLESPOON
INSTANT ESPRESSO
POWDER**

**3 TO 4 TABLESPOONS
HOT WATER**

**2 TABLESPOONS
(1 OUNCE) BUTTER,
MELTED**

**1 CUP
CONFECTIONERS'
SUGAR, OR MORE
AS NEEDED**

Mix the instant espresso powder and hot water together in a medium bowl. Add the melted butter and sugar. Add more of this or that to get the mix just how you like, including more espresso powder for a stronger coffee flavor.

Mix&Match with Our Favorite Chocolate Cake (page 85) or Our Favorite Vanilla Cake (page 84)

SOUR CREAM TOPPING

![INGREDIENTS]

1 CUP SOUR CREAM

**2 TABLESPOONS
PLUS 1 TEASPOON
SUGAR**

**½ TEASPOON
VANILLA EXTRACT**

What, you may ask, is this? Well, do you like the sour cream top that comes on New York–style cheesecake? I could eat it by the bowlful! It's a really great topping to add to a slice of certain cakes, especially alongside fresh berries.

Makes 1 cup

Combine all the ingredients in a small bowl and stir well. Keep covered and refrigerated until ready to use. Use as a garnish just before serving.

Mix&Match with Sour Cream and Berry Cake (page 91), Apple Passover Cake (page 89), or Apple Pie (page 115)

WHIPPED CREAM

INGREDIENTS

1 TO 2 TABLESPOONS GRANULATED SUGAR OR CONFECTIONERS' SUGAR

1 CUP HEAVY WHIPPING CREAM

½ TEASPOON VANILLA EXTRACT

Fresh whipped cream at your service! A few tips that really help: Make sure the bowl is very clean. Put the bowl and paddle or whisk in the refrigerator or freezer for at least 15 minutes before you begin. Most important, be sure not to overbeat the cream.

Makes about 2 cups

1 If using granulated sugar, combine the sugar, cream, and vanilla and chill the mixture for 30 minutes before whipping the cream in a bowl or mixer. Whip until stiff peaks form. Chill until ready to use.

If using confectioners' sugar, beat the cream by itself until it starts to thicken, then add the confectioners' sugar and vanilla and continue beating until stiff peaks form. Chill until ready to use.

2 Use to top your favorite desserts. I think whipped cream is best used right away, but it can last a day or two.

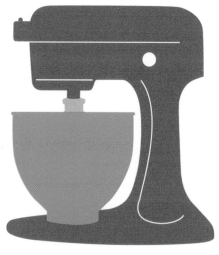

TREATS ARE GOOD! TREATS ARE GOOD! TREATS ARE GOOD! TREATS ARE GOOD! TREATS ARE GOOD! TREATS ARE GOOD! TREATS ARE GOOD! TREATS ARE GOOD! TREATS ARE GOOD! TRE
RE GOOD! TREATS ARE GOOD! TREATS ARE GOOD! TREATS ARE GOOD! TREATS ARE GOOD! TREATS ARE GOOD! TREATS ARE GOOD! TREATS ARE GOOD! TREATS ARE GOOD! TREATS ARE G
TREATS ARE GOOD! TREATS ARE GOOD! TREATS ARE GOOD! TREATS ARE GOOD! TREATS ARE GOOD! TREATS ARE GOOD! TREATS ARE GOOD! TREATS ARE GOOD! TREATS ARE GOOD! TREA
RE GOOD! TREATS ARE GOOD! TREATS ARE GOOD! TREATS ARE GOOD! TREATS ARE GOOD! TREATS ARE GOOD! TREATS ARE GOOD! TREATS ARE GOOD! TREATS ARE GOOD! TREATS ARE GOOD!

CHOCOLATE WHIPPED CREAM

INGREDIENTS

1 CUP HEAVY WHIPPING CREAM

½ CUP CHOPPED DARK CHOCOLATE

1 TABLESPOON SUGAR

½ TEASPOON VANILLA EXTRACT

Yes, that's right! You can use this to dollop on top of a dessert or even frost a whole cake (just double the recipe!). While our recipe calls for dark chocolate, you can also use bittersweet chocolate. If you like it a bit sweeter, add a bit more sugar. Taste along the way and adjust as you wish!

Makes about 2 cups

1   Warm the heavy cream in a saucepan over medium-low heat, stirring it until it is hot. Add the chopped chocolate and sugar and stir until all the chocolate has melted. Take off the heat and mix in the vanilla. Taste to see if it is just the way you like. Yum?

2   Cool the mixture in the fridge until completely chilled.

3   Remember to put the bowl and paddle or whisk in the refrigerator or freezer to chill for at least 15 minutes before you begin to whip the cream.

4   Whip the cream until stiff peaks form.

5   Chill until ready to serve atop your favorite desserts! If using as a frosting for a cake, frost the cake and chill until ready to serve.

ROYAL ICING

Royal icing is a very stiff icing when dry, which makes it perfect for creating details on cookies with no risk of smooshing the icing. Personally, I prefer the taste and texture of buttercream frosting for most cookies, but when you want to make an intricate design with frosting, royal icing is the way to go. I especially recommend it for decorating gingerbread men.

You can make royal icing with egg whites or meringue powder. I prefer to use meringue powder, but both options work nicely! They turn out about the same, but I prefer not to use raw egg whites, and meringue powder is also super-convenient and easy to use. If you want to use egg whites and are concerned about the raw eggs, you can buy pasteurized egg whites at the supermarket.

There are two kinds of decorating using royal icing: outlining and flooding. For outlining, which is creating an outline or a fine line detail on a cookie, you'll need a stiffer icing. For flooding (filling a larger area with icing), you'll need a looser icing. Just add a little more or less water or sugar depending on how stiff you need your icing to be.

And of course you can mix in food coloring to give yourself lots of fun options!

THE MAGIC OF MERINGUE WASH

Meringue powder is one of my favorite toys in the kitchen. Basically, meringue powder is dried egg whites. You can buy a jar of it at most baking supply stores or order it online. Along with its use in royal icing, you can use it just like glue for decorating sugar cookies with sprinkles. I think it's magic. Just mix a little meringue powder with water to make a meringue wash. With a small pastry brush, brush a little wash on the cookies before you decorate them with sprinkles and sugar. The wash will dry and keep the sprinkles and sanding sugar in place, just like magic.

ROYAL ICING MADE WITH MERINGUE POWDER

INGREDIENTS

Makes 2½ cups

¼ CUP MERINGUE
POWDER

2 CUPS
(16 OUNCES) SIFTED
CONFECTIONERS'
SUGAR

1 TEASPOON
VANILLA EXTRACT

1   Using a whisk, beat the meringue powder and ½ cup water in a large bowl until frothy. Slowly whisk in the sugar, then the vanilla. Add more water if the icing seems too stiff or more sugar if the icing seems too loose. Remember to keep the royal icing covered when you're not using it so that it doesn't dry out.

2   Put the royal icing in a piping bag with a small tip for decorating. When piping an outline on a cookie, allow it to dry for a few minutes before flooding. For flooding, use a butter knife, a small offset icing spatula, or even the back of a spoon to spread the thinner royal icing. Also, a toothpick is great for getting the icing into corners!

3   Allow time for the icing to dry before serving the cookies or packing them in a box.

ROYAL ICING MADE WITH EGG WHITES

INGREDIENTS

Makes almost 1 cup

2 LARGE EGG WHITES

2 TEASPOONS FRESH
LEMON JUICE

2 CUPS
CONFECTIONERS'
SUGAR

Using an electric mixer or a hand mixer, beat the egg whites and lemon juice together in a large bowl. Add the confectioners' sugar and continue mixing until you get the consistency you desire. Remember to cover the icing if you're not using it right away!

SANDING SUGAR & SPRINKLES

These guys bring the world a whole lot of good cheer. People of all ages love sprinkles and sanding sugar, the sparkly bigger crystals. Sprinkles and sugar add pizzazz and spirit as only they can. A flower-shaped sugar cookie with brightly colored sugar is such a cheerful thing, and a cupcake with sprinkles on top is sure to bring a smile.

HERE ARE MY FAVORITES TO USE:

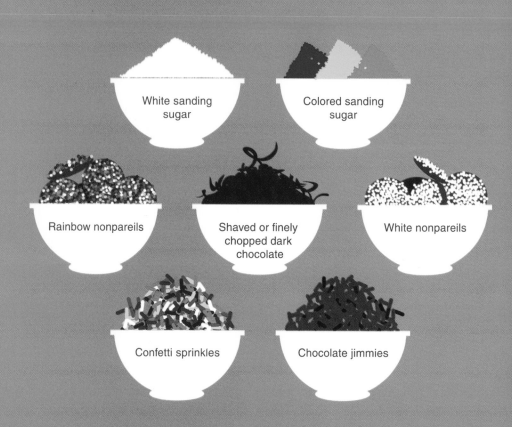

White sanding sugar

Colored sanding sugar

Rainbow nonpareils

Shaved or finely chopped dark chocolate

White nonpareils

Confetti sprinkles

Chocolate jimmies

CAKES & CUPCAKES

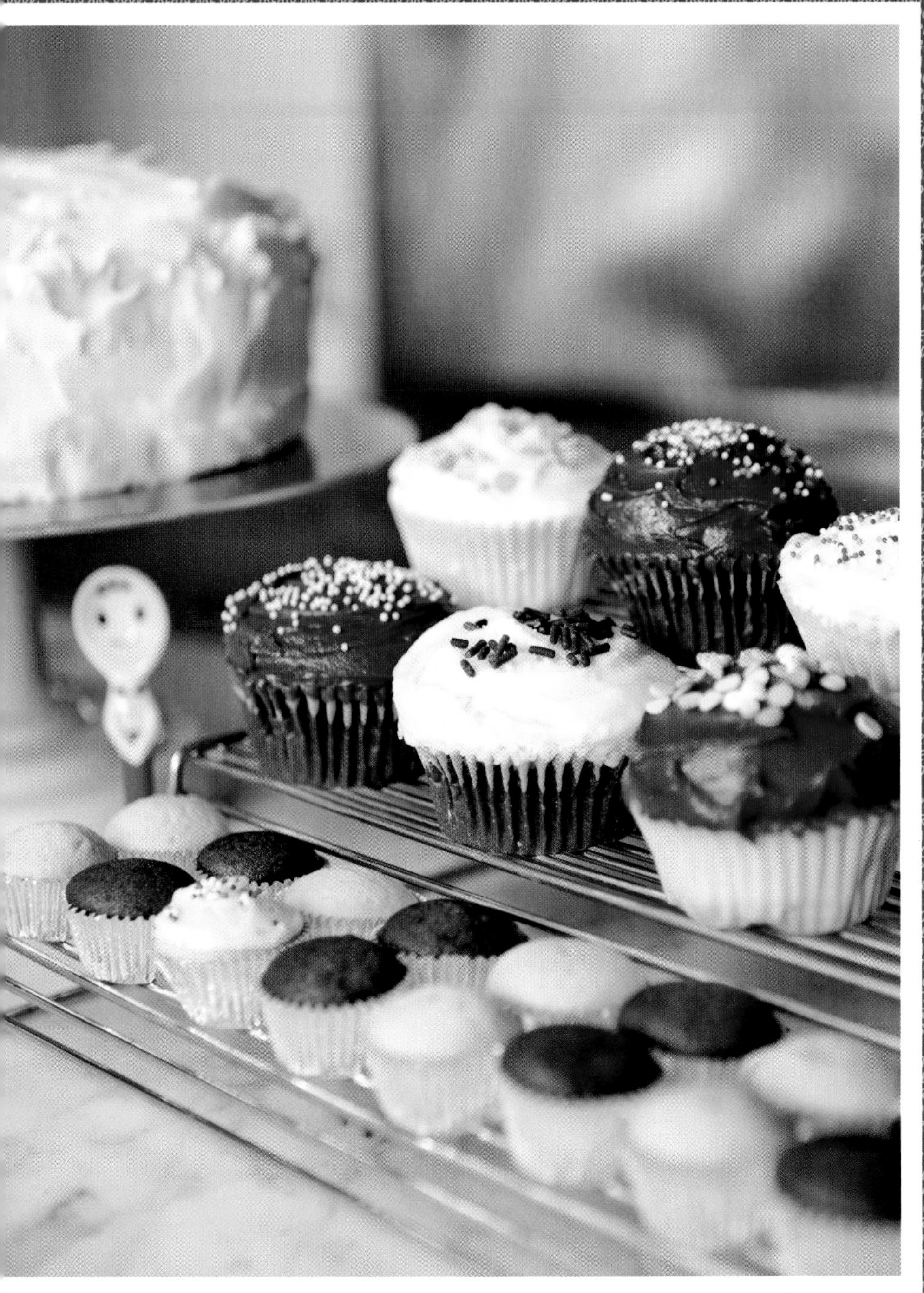

Cake is delicious
and festive.
I love cake.

*Note: These cake recipes can be made as cakes or cupcakes, and you can **Mix & Match** cakes and frostings as you wish! In general, one 9 by 13-inch pan = two 9-inch round pans = 24 cupcakes. If a recipe makes less than that, you can usually double it to get the size you wish.*

When I think of cakes and cupcakes, I think of birthday parties, graduation parties, and special dinners. I associate all kinds of celebrations with cakes, and isn't it fun for friends and family to figure out the perfect cake for a particular special occasion?

I also have fond memories of cake and coffee with friends and neighbors. Having someone over for coffee and cake is special and lovely and a break from our usual days of rushing around. I think cakes help us slow down and put our feet up, so to speak.

Cupcakes, on the other hand, are great on the go, so portable and easy to serve. Whether for a party or as a snack in the middle of a busy day, a cupcake is a delightful treat. And then there are ice cream cone cupcakes, which hold a special place in my heart. Do you know about ice cream cone cupcakes? Just you wait! We're big fans of cone cakes at The Treats Truck!

So here's to cakes of all sizes and shapes and all the ways they help us celebrate.

TREATS ARE GOOD! TREATS ARE GOOD!

OUR FAVORITE VANILLA CAKE

INGREDIENTS

¾ CUP (1½ STICKS) BUTTER

1 CUP PLUS 2 TABLESPOONS SUGAR

4 EGGS

2¼ CUPS FLOUR

2¼ TEASPOONS BAKING POWDER

⅜ TEASPOON SALT

¾ CUP WHOLE MILK

2 TEASPOONS VANILLA EXTRACT

A good old-fashioned vanilla cake is about as good as it gets, in my opinion. And you can match it with chocolate frosting, or a generous layer of buttercream, or many different frostings and toppings; so go crazy! (Although sometimes a vanilla cupcake with vanilla frosting and sprinkles is just the best thing ever.)

Makes a double-layer 9-inch round cake, one 9 by 13-inch cake, or 24 cupcakes

1   Preheat the oven to 350°F. Grease two 9-inch round pans or one 9 by 13-inch pan, or place cupcake papers in a 24-cup cupcake pan.

2   In a large bowl or mixer, cream the butter and sugar until fluffy. Add in the eggs, one at at time.

3   In a separate bowl, mix together the flour, baking powder, and salt.

4   In a measuring cup, combine the milk and vanilla.

5   Add the flour mixture little by little to the butter mixture, alternating with the milk and vanilla and mixing as you go. Do not overmix.

6   Pour the batter into the prepared pan and bake for 30 to 35 minutes (18 to 20 minutes for cupcakes), or until a toothpick comes out clean.

7   Cool the cake completely before removing from the pan. Run a butter knife along the edges to help ease the cake out of the pan. Ice with the frosting of your choice!

Mix&Match with

Buttercream Frosting (page 60),

Chocolate Frosting (page 61), or

Lemony Lemon Frosting (page 62)

Tip: Using a crumb coat is a great technique for beautifully frosting a cake.

Coat a thin layer of frosting all over your cake. Refrigerate the cake to let the frosting set for 30 minutes or more. Take the cake out and add another layer of frosting over the crumb coat. Your cake will be a beauty!

TREATS ARE GOOD! TREATS ARE GOOD! TREATS ARE GOOD! TREATS ARE GOOD! TREATS ARE GOOD! TREATS ARE GOOD! TREATS ARE GOOD! TREATS ARE GOOD! TREATS ARE GOOD! TREATS ARE GOOD! TREATS ARE GOOD! TREATS ARE GOOD! TREATS ARE GOOD! TREATS ARE GOOD! TREATS ARE GOOD! TREATS ARE GOOD! TREATS ARE GOOD! TREATS ARE GOOD! TREATS ARE GOOD! TRE

OUR FAVORITE CHOCOLATE CAKE

INGREDIENTS

1½ CUPS (3 STICKS) BUTTER

2½ CUPS SUGAR

4 EGGS

2¾ CUPS FLOUR

1 TEASPOON BAKING SODA

1 TEASPOON SALT

1 CUP COCOA POWDER

1 TABLESPOON PLUS 1 TEASPOON INSTANT ESPRESSO POWDER

2 CUPS MILK

1 TABLESPOON PLUS 1 TEASPOON VANILLA EXTRACT

Mix&Match with

Chocolate Frosting (page 61),

Buttercream Frosting (page 60),

Chocolate Ganache (page 64), or

Candy Frosting (page 67)

I believe I just said that a vanilla cake was about as good as it gets. Well . . . I'm going to amend that thought and say that chocolate cake takes its rightful place alongside vanilla cake as the king and queen of as good as it gets! Come on, chocolate cake? What would birthdays be without chocolate cake? And, like vanilla cake, it matches up with so many wonderful frostings. Long live the king and queen!

Makes a double-layer 9-inch round cake, one 9 by 13-inch cake, or 24 cupcakes

1   Preheat the oven to 350°F. Grease and dust with flour two 9-inch round pans or one 9 by 13-inch pan, or place cupcake papers in a 24-cup cupcake pan.

2   In a large bowl or mixer, cream the butter and sugar until fluffy. Add in the eggs, one at a time.

3   In a separate bowl, mix together the flour, baking soda, salt, cocoa powder, and instant espresso.

4   In a measuring cup, combine the milk and vanilla.

5   Add the flour mixture little by little to the butter mixture, alternating with the milk and vanilla and mixing as you go. Do not overmix.

6   Pour the batter into the prepared pan and bake for 30 to 35 minutes (18 to 20 minutes for cupcakes), or until a toothpick comes out clean.

7   Cool the cake completely before removing from the pan. Run a butter knife along the edges to help ease the cake out of the pan. Ice with the frosting of your choice!

TREATS ARE GOOD! TREATS ARE GOOD! TREATS ARE GOOD! TREATS ARE GOOD! TREATS ARE GOOD! TREATS ARE GOOD! TREATS ARE GOOD! TREATS ARE GOOD! TREATS ARE GOOD! TRE
RE GOOD! TREATS ARE GOOD! TREATS ARE GOOD! TREATS ARE GOOD! TREATS ARE GOOD! TREATS ARE GOOD! TREATS ARE GOOD! TREATS ARE GOOD! TREATS ARE GOOD! TREATS ARE G
TREATS ARE GOOD! TREATS ARE GOOD! TREATS ARE GOOD! TREATS ARE GOOD! TREATS ARE GOOD! TREATS ARE GOOD! TREATS ARE GOOD! TREATS ARE GOOD! TREATS ARE GOOD! TREATS ARE G
RE GOOD! TREATS ARE GOOD! TREATS ARE GOOD! TREATS ARE GOOD! TREATS ARE GOOD! TREATS ARE GOOD! TREATS ARE GOOD! TREATS ARE GOOD! TREATS ARE GOOD! TREATS ARE GOOD! TRE

CARROT CAKE

INGREDIENTS

**1 POUND CARROTS
(6 OR 7 LARGE
CARROTS), PEELED**

2½ CUPS FLOUR

**1¼ TEASPOONS
BAKING POWDER**

**1 TEASPOON
BAKING SODA**

**1¼ TEASPOONS
GROUND CINNAMON**

**½ TEASPOON
GROUND NUTMEG**

**⅛ TEASPOON
GROUND CLOVES**

½ TEASPOON SALT

**1½ CUPS
CONFECTIONERS'
SUGAR**

**½ CUP PACKED
DARK BROWN SUGAR**

**1¼ CUPS
VEGETABLE OIL**

**4 EGGS, LIGHTLY
BEATEN**

We serve a lot of carrot cake with cream cheese frosting. People love the moist cake with the creamy frosting—and, from our informal polling, our customers prefer their carrot cake without raisins or nuts and with lots and lots of cream cheese frosting!

Makes a double-layer 9-inch round cake, one 9 by 13-inch cake, or 24 cupcakes

1   Preheat the oven to 350°F. Grease two 9-inch round pans or one 9 by 13-inch pan or with cooking spray or oil. In addition, you can also place a cut-out parchment circle on the bottom of the pan.

2   Grate the carrots with a grater (the old-school way!) or a food processor. I prefer medium-grated carrots—not too big, not too fine.

3   In a large bowl, mix together the flour, baking powder, baking soda, cinnamon, nutmeg, cloves, salt, confectioners' sugar, and brown sugar. Stir in the oil and eggs, then the carrots.

4   Pour the batter into the prepared pan and bake for 30 to 40 minutes, or until a toothpick comes out clean.

5   Cool completely, then frost with cream cheese frosting.

Mix&Match with

Cream Cheese
Frosting (page 63)

BANANA CAKE

INGREDIENTS

½ CUP (1 STICK)
BUTTER, MELTED

2 EGGS

1½ CUPS MASHED
BANANAS

½ TEASPOON
VANILLA EXTRACT

1½ CUPS FLOUR

¾ CUP SUGAR

1 TEASPOON BAKING
POWDER

½ TEASPOON
BAKING SODA

¼ TEASPOON SALT

FROSTING OR GLAZE
OF YOUR CHOICE

The big debate with this cake for me is how to eat it—plain, or with buttercream frosting, chocolate frosting, or cream cheese frosting. It's hard to choose and they're all so good. And will I share or keep it all for myself?

Makes one 8- or 9-inch round cake or one 8-inch loaf (double the recipe to make two 9-inch round cakes)

1   Preheat the oven to 350°F and grease an 8- or 9-inch round cake pan or an 8-inch loaf pan.

2   In a medium bowl, combine the butter, eggs, bananas, and vanilla.

3   In a large bowl, combine the flour, sugar, baking powder, baking soda, and salt.

4   Make a well in the dry ingredients. Pour in the wet ingredients and mix just enough to incorporate.

5   Pour the batter into the pan and bake for 35 to 45 minutes, or until a toothpick comes out clean.

6   Cool the cake completely before frosting.

Mix&Match with

Buttercream
Frosting (page 60),

Chocolate Frosting
(page 61),

Cream Cheese
Frosting 63), or

Chocolate Glaze
(page 72)

VARIATION: ADD CHOCOLATE CHIPS TO THE BATTER FOR A CHOCOLATE CHIP BANANA CAKE.

APPLE PASSOVER CAKE

INGREDIENTS

CAKE

3 EGGS

1½ CUPS VEGETABLE OIL

1½ CUPS WHITE SUGAR

2¼ CUPS MATZO CAKE MEAL (OR PLAIN MATZOS GROUND IN A BLENDER OR FOOD PROCESSOR)

¾ CUP POTATO STARCH

1½ TEASPOONS GROUND CINNAMON

FILLING

6 LARGE APPLES, PEELED, CORED, AND THINLY SLICED

½ CUP DARK BROWN SUGAR, PLUS EXTRA FOR SPRINKLING

1 TEASPOON GROUND CINNAMON

½ TEASPOON GROUND NUTMEG

I make this leavening-free cake for friends and family and customers around Passover, but it's great any time of the year!

Makes one 9 by 13-inch cake

1   Preheat the oven to 350°F and grease a 9 by 13-inch pan.

2   To make the cake, in a large bowl, whisk together the eggs, oil, and white sugar. Stir in the matzo cake meal, potato starch, and cinnamon.

3   To make the filling, in a separate bowl, toss the apples, brown sugar, cinnamon, and nutmeg.

4   Pour half the cake mixture into the bottom of the pan. Layer the entire apple mixture on top, spreading it evenly over the cake mixture.

5   Pour the rest of the cake mixture on top. Sprinkle with brown sugar.

6   Bake for 45 minutes.

TREATS ARE GOOD! TREATS ARE GOOD! TREATS ARE GOOD! TREATS ARE GOOD! TREATS ARE GOOD! TREATS ARE GOOD! TREATS ARE GOOD! TREATS ARE GOOD! TRE.
TREATS ARE GOOD! TREATS ARE GOOD! TREATS ARE GOOD! TREATS ARE GOOD! TREATS ARE GOOD! TREATS ARE GOOD! TREATS ARE GOOD! TREATS ARE GOOD! TREA
TREATS ARE GOOD! TREATS ARE GOOD! TREATS ARE GOOD! TREATS ARE GOOD! TREATS ARE GOOD! TREATS ARE GOOD! TREATS ARE GOOD! TREATS ARE GO
TREATS ARE GOOD! TREATS ARE GOOD! TREATS ARE GOOD! TREATS ARE GOOD! TREATS ARE GOOD! TREATS ARE GOOD! TREATS ARE GOOD! TREATS ARE GOOD! TREATS ARE GO

LEMON CAKE

INGREDIENTS

1 CUP (2 STICKS)
BUTTER, SOFTENED

1 CUP SUGAR

4 EGGS

1 TEASPOON
VANILLA EXTRACT

ZEST OF 1 LARGE
LEMON

2 CUPS FLOUR

2 TEASPOONS
BAKING POWDER

¼ TEASPOON SALT

½ CUP FRESHLY
SQUEEZED LEMON
JUICE

Mix&Match with

Lemon Glaze
(page 72),

Lemony Lemon
Frosting (page 62),

Lemony Cream
Cheese Frosting
(page 63), or

Coconut Frosting
(page 68)

A nice lemon cake, either frosted or glazed, is such a good reason to have a neighbor or friend stop by for a piece of cake and some much-needed chat. I have to admit a certain weakness for a lemon-glazed lemon cake. The combined charms of cake and icy glaze are joy on a plate.

Makes one 9-inch round cake

1   Preheat the oven to 350°F and grease and dust with flour a 9-inch round pan.

2   In a large bowl or mixer, cream the butter and sugar. Mix in the eggs, one at a time. Mix in the vanilla and lemon zest.

3   In a separate bowl, combine the flour, baking powder, and salt. Add the flour mixture a little at a time to the butter mixture.

4   Add the lemon juice and mix just enough to combine.

5   Pour the batter into the prepared pan and bake for 30 to 40 minutes, or until a toothpick comes out clean.

6   After the cake has cooled in the pan, remove from the pan and frost with the frosting of your choice.

SOUR CREAM AND BERRY CAKE

INGREDIENTS

½ CUP (1 STICK)
BUTTER, SOFTENED

1 CUP WHITE SUGAR

3 EGGS

2 CUPS FLOUR

½ TEASPOON SALT

1 TEASPOON
BAKING POWDER

1 TEASPOON
BAKING SODA

1 CUP SOUR CREAM

1 TEASPOON
VANILLA EXTRACT

2 CUPS BERRIES
(OPTIONAL: AN
EXTRA CUP OF
BERRIES TO GARNISH
THE PLATE WHEN
SERVING)

½ CUP DARK
BROWN SUGAR

This is a great afternoon-with-tea kind of cake or a great
dessert for a brunch. It's best served either plain or with
some fresh berries and whipped cream or sour cream
topping. You can use one kind of berries or a mix. I like to
use a mix of raspberries, blueberries, and blackberries, with
more fresh berries on the side.

Makes one 9 by 13-inch cake

1   Preheat the oven to 325°F. Grease and dust with flour a
    9 by 13-inch pan.

2   In a mixer or a big bowl, cream the butter and white sugar.
    Mix in the eggs, one at a time.

3   In another bowl, combine the flour, salt, baking powder,
    and baking soda.

4   Gradually add the flour mixture to the butter mixture,
    alternating with adding the sour cream until fully combined.

5   Stir in the vanilla and 1 cup of the berries.

6   Pour half the batter into the pan. Sprinkle the rest of the
    berries all over the batter and sprinkle the brown sugar on
    top. Pour the remaining batter evenly over the berries and
    brown sugar.

7   Bake for 45 to 50 minutes, or until a toothpick comes
    out clean.

Mix&Match with

Whipped Cream
(page 74) or

Sour Cream
Topping (page 73)

VARIATION: WALNUT SOUR
CREAM CAKE—INSTEAD OF
BERRIES, MIX 1 CUP FINELY
CHOPPED WALNUTS WITH
THE BROWN SUGAR FOR THE
MIDDLE OF THE CAKE.

91

COCONUT CAKE

INGREDIENTS

1½ CUPS
(2½ STICKS) BUTTER

2 CUPS SUGAR

5 EGGS

2 TEASPOONS
VANILLA EXTRACT

3 CUPS FLOUR

1 TEASPOON BAKING
POWDER

½ TEASPOON
BAKING SODA

½ TEASPOON SALT

1 CUP BUTTERMILK
(SEE NOTE)

1¼ CUPS SHREDDED
SWEETENED
COCONUT

This charmer pairs so well with frosting. The combination of moist coconut cake with creamy frosting makes a great cake or batch of cupcakes!

Makes a double-layer 9-inch round cake, one 9 by 13-inch cake, or 24 cupcakes

1   Preheat the oven to 350°F. Grease and dust with flour two 9-inch round pans, or place cupcake papers in a 24-cup cupcake pan.

2   In a mixer or a large bowl, cream the butter and sugar until light and fluffy. Mix in the eggs, one at a time. Add the vanilla and mix well.

3   In a separate bowl, combine the flour, baking powder, baking soda, and salt. Alternate mixing the flour mixture and the buttermilk into the batter, taking care not to overmix. Fold in the coconut.

4   Pour the batter into the pan and bake for 30 to 40 minutes, or until a toothpick comes out clean.

Mix&Match with Coconut Frosting (page 68), Lemony Cream Cheese Frosting (page 63), Chocolate Frosting (page 61), or Cake Sandwiches (page 138)

Note: To make buttermilk at home, simply add 1 teaspoon white vinegar or lemon juice to 1 cup milk.

POPPY SEED CAKE

DI TREAT
EATS ARE
OOD! TREA
TS ARE GO
OD! TREAT
EATS ARE
OD! TREA
ATS ARE G
DI TREATS
TS ARE GO
RE GOOD!
! TREATS
GOOD! TR
EATS ARE
E GOOD!
TS ARE G
OOD! TREA
EATS ARE
ARE GOOD
GOOD! TR
EATS ARE
DI TREATS
GOOD! TR
TS ARE GO
GOOD! TR
EATS ARE
OOD! TRE
RE GOOD!
DI TREATS
TREATS AF
E GOOD! T
TS ARE GO
DI TREATS
REATS ARE
RE GOOD!
EATS ARE
DI TREATS
EATS ARE
OODI TRE
TS ARE GO
DI TREATS
ATS ARE G
ARE GOOL
TS ARE GO
TREATS A
EATS ARE
GOOD! TR
DI TREATS
GOOD! TR
EATS ARE
E GOOD! T
TS ARE GO
DDI TREAT
EATS ARE
OD! TREAT
TS ARE GO
DOI TREA
EATS ARE
RE GOOD!
S ARE GOO
DODI TREA
S ARE GOO
RE GOOD!
ARE GOO
GOOD! TR
TREATS AR
E GOOD! TI
EATS ARE
ODI TREAT
EATS ARE
GOOD! TR
TREATS A
OODI TRE
ATS ARE G
GOOD! TRI
EATS ARE
ODI TREAT
ARE GOO
GOOD! TR
REATS AR

INGREDIENTS

½ CUP POPPY SEEDS

1 CUP BUTTERMILK

**2 TEASPOONS
ALMOND EXTRACT
(I LOVE THE ALMOND
FLAVOR, BUT YOU
CAN USE VANILLA
IF YOU PREFER)**

2½ CUPS FLOUR

**1 TEASPOON
BAKING POWDER**

**1 TEASPOON
BAKING SODA**

½ TEASPOON SALT

**1 CUP (2 STICKS)
BUTTER**

1¾ CUPS SUGAR

4 EGGS, SEPARATED

If you want to eat this cake while it's still warm from the oven, you most certainly can. Just thinking of a warm, just-out-of-the-oven slice of cake makes me want to head straight to the kitchen and start baking one now . . .

Makes a 9-inch round cake or one 9-inch square cake

1 Preheat the oven to 350°F. Grease and dust with flour a 9-inch round or square pan.

2 In a small bowl, combine the poppy seeds, buttermilk, and almond extract and set aside. If you have the time, do this step an hour or two in advance, to give the poppy seeds a chance to soften.

3 In a medium bowl, combine the flour, baking powder, baking soda, and salt.

4 In a large bowl, beat the butter and 1½ cups of the sugar. Add the egg yolks and beat well. Stir the poppy seed mixture into the butter and egg yolk mixture. Mix in the flour mixture until thoroughly combined.

5 In a clean mixer or large bowl, beat the egg whites until soft peaks form. Add the remaining ¼ cup sugar and beat until stiff peaks form.

6 Gently fold the egg white mixture into the batter.

7 Pour the batter into the prepared pan and bake for 35 to 45 minutes, or until a toothpick comes out clean. This cake is delicious served plain or frosted or glazed.

Mix&Match with Chocolate Glaze (page 72), Lemon Glaze (page 72), Lemony Lemon Frosting (page 62), or Lemony Cream Cheese Frosting (page 63)

DEVIL'S FOOD CAKE

INGREDIENTS

2 CUPS FLOUR

1 TEASPOON SALT

1 TEASPOON BAKING POWDER

2 TEASPOONS BAKING SODA

¾ CUP COCOA POWDER

2 CUPS SUGAR

1 CUP VEGETABLE OIL

1 CUP HOT COFFEE

1 CUP MILK

2 EGGS

1 TEASPOON VANILLA EXTRACT

This is one of my favorite cakes to make for birthdays. It's so moist and so good, especially when frosted with buttercream frosting.

Makes a double-layer 9-inch round cake, one 9 by 13-inch cake, or 24 cupcakes

1   Preheat the oven to 350°F. Grease two 9-inch round pans or one 9 by 13-inch pan.

2   In a mixer or large bowl, combine the flour, salt, baking powder, baking soda, cocoa powder, and sugar. Add the vegetable oil, coffee, and milk and mix until combined. Mix in the eggs and vanilla.

3   Pour the batter into the prepared pan and bake for 30 to 40 minutes, or until a toothpick comes out clean.

Mix&Match with

Buttercream Frosting (page 60),

Chocolate Glaze (page 72), or

Chocolate Frosting (page 61)

TREATS ARE GOOD! TREATS ARE GOOD! TREATS ARE GOOD! TREATS ARE GOOD! TREATS ARE GOOD! TREATS ARE GOOD! TREATS ARE GOOD! TREATS ARE GOOD! TREATS ARE GOOD! TRE
RE GOOD! TREATS ARE GOOD! TREATS ARE GOOD! TREATS ARE GOOD! TREATS ARE GOOD! TREATS ARE GOOD! TREATS ARE GOOD! TREATS ARE GOOD! TREATS ARE GOOD! TREATS ARE (
TREATS ARE GOOD! TREATS ARE GOOD! TREATS ARE GOOD! TREATS ARE GOOD! TREATS ARE GOOD! TREATS ARE GOOD! TREATS ARE GOOD! TREATS ARE GOOD! TREATS ARE GOOD! TREATS ARE (
E GOOD! TREATS ARE GOOD! TREATS ARE GOOD! TREATS ARE GOOD! TREATS ARE GOOD! TREATS ARE GOOD! TREATS ARE GOOD! TREATS ARE GOOD! TREATS ARE GOOD! TREATS ARE GOOD! TREATS ARE GO

CUPCAKES

INGREDIENTS

CAKE BATTER

FROSTING

SPRINKLES

Cupcakes are great for all kinds of occasions, including parties. They are the perfect little portable piece of cake. We make lots of vanilla and chocolate cupcakes, and sometimes carrot or pumpkin or devil's food. Lemon and coconut are also favorites. You can make cupcakes with any cake recipe—just follow the directions below! Cupcakes are best when freshly baked, so I recommend baking the same day you serve them or just the night before.

1 Preheat the oven to 350°F. Place cupcake liners in a cupcake pan and fill them two-thirds full of cake batter. Bake the cupcakes for 18 to 20 minutes, or until a toothpick comes out clean.

2 Cool the cupcakes before adding frosting and sprinkles.

Note: Mini-cupcakes are great, too. Use mini-cupcake liners and bake for 5 to 7 minutes less than larger cupcakes. A piping bag is a big help for icing these little guys.

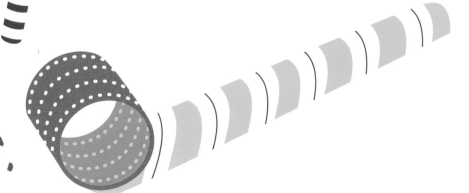

TODAY'S SPECIAL IS:

really really good!

LET'S SEE WHAT'S JUST AROUND THE CORNER.

ANYTHING GOES IN
Cupcake Cone Land!

WHAT'S AN ICE CREAM CONE CUPCAKE?

A cupcake in an ice cream cone! I had them at parties when I was a kid. I loved them. The cupcakes were baked directly in the cone. When I started The Treats Truck, I couldn't wait to try them out on the truck. One day I had an idea—why don't we try layering the cake and frosting (and cake and more frosting) in the cone? Our customers gave it their very enthusiastic stamp of approval. A vanilla chocolate swirl? A vanilla vanilla cone with gobs of icing and layers of cake? I love a good mint chocolate cone myself!

ICE CREAM CONE CUPCAKES

INGREDIENTS

CAKE BATTER

WAFER ICE CREAM CONES (THE FLAT-BOTTOMED ONES)

FROSTING

SPRINKLES

There are two ways to make ice cream cone cupcakes. Growing up, I had them baked in the cone with the frosting on top. On the truck, we use the layer method in order to get frosting throughout the cone.

Cone cakes are best when made the same day you'll serve them. Bake the cake a day ahead of time, if you'd like. Have your cake and frosting ready to go, and then making cone cakes when you want is a snap! You'll wow your friends with this one—they'll feel very special, indeed!

Here are the directions for both methods. And be sure to use sprinkles! Everything is better with sprinkles!

Note: **Keep the ice cream cone cupcakes in the refrigerator if you don't plan on serving them right away. Take them out 30 to 60 minutes before you want to serve them.**

TIP: I USE A POPOVER PAN TO HOLD THE CONE CAKES.

Popover pans are deep enough to hold the cones and keep them from falling over. If you don't have a popover pan, you can use a cupcake or muffin pan. The cupcake shape is too wide, so make a smaller base by making an aluminum foil ring inside each cup. The cone should fit nice and snug so it doesn't fall over. For traveling with your cones to a party, you can put each cone snugly in a paper cup with a little foil or a napkin for padding and pack all the cups in a box or container.

TREATS ARE GOOD! TREATS ARE GOOD! TREATS ARE GOOD! TREATS ARE GOOD! TREATS ARE GOOD! TREATS ARE GOOD! TREATS ARE GOOD! TREATS ARE GOOD! TREATS ARE GOOD! TREATS ARE GOOD! TREATS ARE GOOD! TREATS ARE GOOD! TREATS ARE GOOD! TREATS ARE GOOD! TREATS ARE GOOD! TRE
I TREATS ARE GOOD! TREATS ARE GOOD! TREATS ARE GOOD! TREATS ARE GOOD! TREATS ARE GOOD! TREATS ARE GOOD! TREATS ARE GOOD! TREATS ARE GOOD! TREATS ARE GOOD! TRE
RE GOOD! TREATS ARE GOOD! TREATS ARE GOOD! TREATS ARE GOOD! TREATS ARE GOOD! TREATS ARE GOOD! TREATS ARE GOOD! TREATS ARE GOOD! TREATS ARE GOOD! TREATS

CLASSIC

1. Place the cones in a cupcake or muffin pan, with a foil base in each cup to keep the cones upright (see Tip).

2. Fill the cones about two-thirds full of batter.

3. Bake the cones for 20 minutes at 350°F.

4. Cool, frost the tops, and add sprinkles.

DELUXE

1. Bake a cake (one 9-inch round cake will do, so half of most of our cake recipes would fit the bill). Or make a 9 by 13-inch cake and have the leftovers for snacks or cake sandwiches!

2. Use a small round cookie cutter to cut out rounds of cake. If you don't have a small cookie cutter, cut little cubes of cake to fit into the cones.

3. Frost the inside of each cone. Be sure to get frosting in the very bottom of the cone. Put one piece of cake in the bottom of the cone. Add a layer of frosting.

4. More cake. More frosting. Two or three little pieces of cake in each cone is plenty. Ice the top of the cone to look like a scoop of ice cream.

5. Sprinkles!

CHEESECAKE

INGREDIENTS

This is a very simple cheesecake recipe. I love it. Just a plain slice always hits the spot, but sometimes a little topping is extra nice. Fresh berries, chocolate sauce, whipped cream—they're all great!

Makes one 9-inch round cake

GRAHAM CRACKER CRUST

1½ CUPS GRAHAM CRACKER CRUMBS

2 TABLESPOONS SUGAR

¼ CUP (4 TABLESPOONS) BUTTER, MELTED

CHEESECAKE FILLING

FIVE 8-OUNCE PACKAGES CREAM CHEESE, AT ROOM TEMPERATURE

1½ CUPS SUGAR

5 EGGS

3 TABLESPOONS FLOUR

⅛ TEASPOON SALT

1 TEASPOON VANILLA EXTRACT

1 TEASPOON LEMON JUICE

½ CUP SOUR CREAM

1   Place a pan filled halfway with water on the bottom rack of the oven. Preheat the oven to 325°F and grease a 9-inch springform pan.

2   To make the graham cracker crust, combine the graham cracker crumbs, sugar, and butter and press the mixture into the bottom of the pan. Bake for 10 minutes, then set aside to cool.

3   To make the filling, in a large bowl or mixer, beat the cream cheese until creamy and smooth. Mix in the other ingredients in this order, taking care not to overmix: sugar, eggs, flour, salt, vanilla, lemon juice, and sour cream. Pour the mixture into the prepared pan.

4   Place the pan on the rack above the pan filled with water and bake for 1 hour 15 minutes to 1 hour 30 minutes. The center of the cake may look slightly soft but will firm up.

5   As soon as you take the cheesecake out of the oven, run a knife along the edge of the pan to loosen the cake from the pan. Allow the cake to cool completely in the pan before refrigerating. Chill for many hours to overnight.

6   Before serving, let the cheesecake sit out for 30 minutes. It will keep in the fridge for up to 4 days.

7   If serving with fresh strawberries, consider tossing the sliced berries in a little sugar at least 20 minutes before you serve them. They'll be extra delicious and a little syrupy, which works perfectly with cheesecake!

PUMPKIN CAKE

3½ CUPS FLOUR

1 TABLESPOON BAKING POWDER

1½ TEASPOONS BAKING SODA

1½ TEASPOONS SALT

2 TABLESPOONS GROUND CINNAMON

1½ TEASPOONS GROUND GINGER

1 TEASPOON GROUND CLOVES

6 EGGS

1¼ CUPS VEGETABLE OIL

1 POUND 6½ OUNCES PUMPKIN PUREE (NOT PIE FILLING)

2½ CUPS SUGAR

Like carrot cake, this one is a real winner with a thick layer of cream cheese frosting on top! And both pumpkin and carrot cake make great cupcakes, too.

Makes a double-layer 9-inch round cake, one 9 by 13-inch cake, or 24 cupcakes

1   Preheat the oven to 350°F and grease a 9 by 13-inch pan or two 9-inch round pans with cooking spray or oil. In addition, you can also place a cut-out parchment circle on the bottom of the pan.

2   In one bowl, mix the flour, baking powder, baking soda, salt, cinnamon, ginger, and cloves. Set aside.

3   In another bowl, mix the eggs, oil, and pumpkin puree. Add the sugar.

4   Mix the dry ingredients with the pumpkin mixture.

5   Pour the batter into the pan and bake for 30 to 40 minutes, or until a toothpick comes out clean.

6   Cool completely, then frost with a generous layer of cream cheese frosting.

Mix&Match with

Cream Cheese
Frosting (page 63)

PIES

I love pie.

For the truck, we make a lot of what I call Jr. Pies, small pies just right for one person, like a cupcake! You can get little pie tins, or if you don't have little tins, bake little pies in a muffin or cupcake pan. Of course, a big old-fashioned pie is always good, especially at home, so there's plenty to go around and hopefully even leftovers (breakfast, anyone?).

Yum. Pie.

**Big pies. Little pies. Pies à la mode.
Let's say it one more time. Pie.**

TIP: FOR COOLING PIES, IT'S BEST TO PLACE THEM ON A WIRE RACK!

PIECRUSTS

For pie lovers, the crust is a very important part of the equation. The contrast of crust and filling is what makes the pie so good. With a few basic pie crust recipes at the ready, you'll be all set to bake! Here's your basic butter crust, and some great cookie crusts, too!

TIP: WHAT'S BEST TO USE TO CUT THE BUTTER INTO THE FLOUR?

You can use two butter knives or a fork, or pulse gently with your mixer, or use your fingers. If you want to get a fun and fancy tool, get a pastry blender, also called a pastry cutter. It's a handheld tool, kind of like a potato masher for pastry dough! Whatever you use, I recommend chilling the utensil in the freezer first, so it's nice and cold! It is important that the butter stays as cold as possible, so if you use your fingers, be careful not to warm the butter too much with your hands.

BLIND BAKING

If you're going to use a butter crust with a recipe that doesn't require baking the filling, you need to prebake or "blind bake" the crust. Put the rolled-out pie dough in the pie pan and chill for at least 15 minutes. When you're ready to bake the crust, prick holes in the crust with a fork. Put a layer of parchment paper, aluminum foil, or a paper coffee filter on top of the crust. Weigh it down with pie weights, dry beans, or uncooked rice. Bake at 425°F for about 10 minutes. Take out the weights and remove the lining. Bake for another 10 to 15 minutes, or until golden brown and fully baked. Set aside until ready to fill!

BUTTER CRUST

INGREDIENTS

2½ CUPS FLOUR

1 TEASPOON SALT

1 TEASPOON SUGAR

1 CUP (2 STICKS)
VERY COLD BUTTER,
CUBED OR CUT INTO
SMALL PIECES

6 TO 8 TABLESPOONS
ICE COLD WATER

OPTIONAL: EGG
WASH (1 EGG
WHISKED WITH
1 TABLESPOON
WATER OR MILK)

Mix&Match with
any recipe you
choose!

A few simple tips will help you make a wonderful butter crust. Make sure the ingredients are very cold—you can even chill the flour! Also, make sure not to overwork the dough—that's really the key. And enjoy! For me, the process of making the dough and assembling a pie can be such a lovely pleasure in itself.

*Makes two 9-inch piecrusts or 12 to 15
Jr. Pie piecrust rounds*

1   In a large bowl or mixer, combine the flour, salt, and sugar. Add the butter pieces and cut them into the flour mixture, working until you have big crumbs (see Tip). Add ice cold water, 1 tablespoon at a time, and mix in until the dough holds together.

2   Divide the dough into 2 mounds. Wrap each mound in plastic wrap and refrigerate for 45 minutes to overnight. Let the dough stand for at least 15 minutes before rolling it out.

3   Roll out the dough on a lightly floured surface or between 2 pieces of parchment or wax paper, then place the rolled-out dough in the pie pan and press into place.

4   For pies with tops, brush a little water on the edges of the bottom crust before adding the top crust and crimp the edges of the top and bottom crusts together with your fingers to seal them all around the pie. You can use your fingers, thumb, fork, or the back of a teaspoon to add a design along the ridges. Also, gently lift the edges from the pan a bit (it helps make it easier to cut and serve slices of the baked pie later on). Make little slits in the top crust to allow steam to escape (and add a decorative charm!). Another fun flourish is to add to the top crust little pieces of scrap dough cut out in shapes such as flowers or leaves. Brush the top crust with an egg wash, place on the decorative bits, and sprinkle with sanding sugar (or regular sugar) for a sparkly top.

CHOCOLATE COOKIE CRUST

I use one of two chocolate cookie crust recipes, depending on the type of pie I'm making. The classic chocolate cookie crust is a straight-up mix of cookie crumbs, melted butter, and sugar, and the second version replaces the butter and sugar with chocolate ganache. It's a bit more decadent for those times you want a richer chocolate crust. For the cookie crumbs, bake a batch of chocolate cookies ahead of time or use store-bought chocolate wafer cookies.

CLASSIC CHOCOLATE COOKIE CRUST

INGREDIENTS

Makes one 9-inch piecrust

⅓ CUP BUTTER

1 ⅔ CUPS CHOCOLATE COOKIE CRUMBS

1 TABLESPOON SUGAR

1   Preheat the oven to 350°F.

2   Melt the butter in a saucepan or in a microwave oven. In a bowl, mix the cookie crumbs and sugar. Add the melted butter and stir until combined.

3   Press the mixture into the pie tin. Bake for 5 to 10 minutes.

Mix&Match with

Chocolate Pie (page 124),

Ice Cream Pie (page 144), or

Banana Cream Pie (page 123)

VARIATION: ADD A TEASPOON OR TWO OF ESPRESSO POWDER IF YOU WANT A LITTLE COFFEE KICK!

DOUBLE CHOCOLATE COOKIE CRUST

INGREDIENTS

Makes one 9-inch piecrust

1²/₃ CUPS
CHOCOLATE COOKIE
CRUMBS

¼ CUP WARM
CHOCOLATE
GANACHE
(PAGE 64)

In a bowl, mix the cookie crumbs and warm ganache. Press the mixture into a pie tin. No need to bake! Just chill until ready to fill.

Mix&Match with Banana Cream Pie (page 123), Vanilla Cream Pie (page 122), or Ice Cream Pie (page 144)

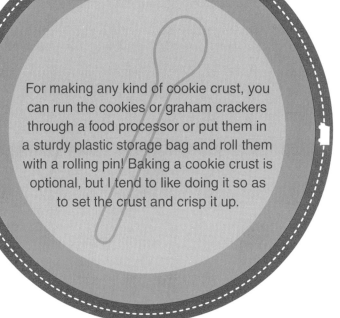

For making any kind of cookie crust, you can run the cookies or graham crackers through a food processor or put them in a sturdy plastic storage bag and roll them with a rolling pin! Baking a cookie crust is optional, but I tend to like doing it so as to set the crust and crisp it up.

GRAHAM CRACKER CRUST

**¼ CUP
(4 TABLESPOONS)
BUTTER**

**1½ CUPS GRAHAM
CRACKER CRUMBS**

**2 TABLESPOONS
SUGAR**

A graham cracker crust can be baked or left unbaked. I prefer to bake it for almost any recipe, as it crisps it up and sets it so nicely.

Makes one 9-inch piecrust

1   Preheat the oven to 350°F (if you're baking—it's optional).

2   Melt the butter in a saucepan or in a microwave oven. In a bowl, mix the graham cracker crumbs and sugar. Add the melted butter and stir until combined. Press the mixture into the pie tin.

3   Bake for 5 to 10 minutes or just refrigerate.

Mix&Match with

Banana Cream Pie
(page 123),

Vanilla Cream Pie
(page 122),

Ice Cream Pie
(page 144),

Cheesecake
(page 102), or

Strawberry Pie
(page 119)

VARIATION: USE GINGERSNAPS INSTEAD OF GRAHAM CRACKERS TO MAKE A GINGERSNAP CRUST!

VARIATION: FOR A RICH, NUTTY FLAVOR, TRY ADDING SOME ALMOND FLOUR OR FINELY CHOPPED ALMONDS TO YOUR CRUST. INSTEAD OF 1½ CUPS OF GRAHAM CRACKER CRUMBS, USE 1 CUP OF GRAHAM CRACKER CRUMBS AND ½ CUP FINELY CHOPPED ALMONDS OR ALMOND FLOUR.

TREATS ARE GOOD! TREATS ARE GOOD! TREATS ARE GOOD! TREATS ARE GOOD! TREATS ARE GOOD! TREATS ARE GOOD! TREATS ARE GOOD! TREATS ARE GOOD! TREATS ARE GOOD! TRE
RE GOOD! TREATS ARE GOOD! TREATS ARE GOOD! TREATS ARE GOOD! TREATS ARE GOOD! TREATS ARE GOOD! TREATS ARE GOOD! TREATS ARE GOOD! TREATS ARE G
TREATS ARE GOOD! TREATS ARE GOOD! TREATS ARE GOOD! TREATS ARE GOOD! TREATS ARE GOOD! TREATS ARE GOOD! TREATS ARE GOOD! TREATS ARE GOOD! TREA
E GOOD! TREATS ARE GOOD! TREATS ARE GOOD! TREATS ARE GOOD! TREATS ARE GOOD! TREATS ARE GOOD! TREATS ARE GOOD! TREATS ARE GOOD! TREATS ARE GO

SHORTBREAD CRUSTS

You can make a shortbread cookie crust following the standard cookie crust recipe using store-bought shortbread cookies, or you can make a homemade shortbread crust that's more like a regular piecrust.

SHORTBREAD COOKIE CRUST

INGREDIENTS

Makes one 9-inch piecrust

¼ CUP
(4 TABLESPOONS)
BUTTER

1 ½ CUPS
SHORTBREAD
COOKIE CRUMBS

1 TABLESPOON
SUGAR

1   Preheat the oven to 350°F (if you're baking—it's optional).

2   Melt the butter in a saucepan or in a microwave oven. In a bowl, mix the cookie crumbs and sugar. Add the melted butter and stir until combined. Press the mixture into the pie tin.

3   Bake for 5 to 10 minutes or just refrigerate.

SHORTBREAD CRUST FROM SCRATCH

INGREDIENTS

Makes one 9-inch piecrust

1 CUP FLOUR

¼ CUP
CONFECTIONERS'
SUGAR

⅛ TEASPOON SALT

½ CUP (1 STICK)
COLD BUTTER

1   Preheat the oven to 425°F. Grease a 9-inch pie pan.

2   In a mixer or a bowl, mix the flour, sugar, and salt. Cut the butter into small pieces and cut them into the flour mixture until small crumbs form. Press the dough into the pie pan.

3   Freeze for 15 minutes or chill for 30 minutes.

4   Prick the crust with a fork before baking. Bake for 10 to 15 minutes, or until golden and baked through.

Mix&Match with Strawberry Pie (page 119) or Peach Pie (page 120)

JR. PIES

Small, cute, and portable, Jr. Pies are great for parties or picnics. We make Jr. Pies for The Treats Truck in little 4-inch pie tins (they come as small as 3 inches and as large as 5 inches). You can buy them online or at a baking supply store. Another option is to use a muffin or cupcake pan. Use foil cupcake papers (which look like pie tins), or just bake them directly in the pan.

For most kinds of Jr. Pies, you just follow the recipe as you would for a big pie, with the exception of apple pie. I recommend cooking the apple filling in a saucepan before baking the pies, to make sure the apples get fully cooked. The baking time will be about half as long as a recipe calls for, but do keep an eye on them—it could be a little less or more!

If you're making Jr. Pies with top crusts, one option is to cut out a small shape (flower or star) that's about the width of the little tin. Place the cutout on top of the pie filling. That way, you get a bit of top crust without it being too heavy. And, I like to use an egg wash and sanding sugar (see page 78), so the little guys have a sparkly top.

TREATS ARE GOOD! TREATS ARE GOOD! TREATS ARE GOOD! TREATS ARE GOOD! TREATS ARE GOOD! TREATS ARE GOOD! TREATS ARE GOOD! TREATS ARE GOOD! TREATS ARE GOOD! TRE
RE GOOD! TREATS ARE GOOD! TREATS ARE GOOD! TREATS ARE GOOD! TREATS ARE GOOD! TREATS ARE GOOD! TREATS ARE GOOD! TREATS ARE GOOD! TREATS ARE GOOD! TREATS
TREATS ARE GOOD! TREATS ARE GOOD! TREATS ARE GOOD! TREATS ARE GOOD! TREATS ARE GOOD! TREATS ARE GOOD! TREATS ARE GOOD! TREATS ARE GOOD! TREATS ARE GOOD! TREATS ARE G

APPLE PIE

**6 TO 7 CUPS APPLE
SLICES (FROM 6 TO
8 APPLES, PEELED,
CORED, AND SLICED)**

**1 TABLESPOON
LEMON JUICE**

**½ TO ¾ CUP WHITE
SUGAR, OR TO TASTE**

**3 TABLESPOONS
FLOUR**

⅛ TEASPOON SALT

**½ TEASPOON
GROUND CINNAMON**

**¼ TEASPOON
GROUND NUTMEG OR
ALLSPICE, OPTIONAL**

**1 BATCH BUTTER
CRUST PIE DOUGH
(PAGE 108)**

**2 TABLESPOONS
BUTTER**

**EGG WASH (PAGE
108), OPTIONAL**

**SANDING SUGAR,
FOR SPRINKLING**

Anytime is a good time for some freshly baked apple pie with whipped cream or a scoop of vanilla ice cream. I like to use a mix of sweet and tart apples, and pick from the best local varieties in season. I sometimes cut out little flowers or leaf shapes with bits of dough to decorate the top crust, and I love to add a sprinkle of clear sanding sugar for a sparkly top.

Makes one 9-inch pie

1   Preheat the oven to 350°F.

2   In a large bowl, toss the apple slices with the lemon juice. In a separate bowl, combine the sugar, flour, salt, cinnamon, and nutmeg or allspice, if using, then stir this mixture into the apples. Set aside.

3   Roll out the pie dough and place the bottom crust in the pie pan.

4   Pour the apples into the pie pan. Dot with the butter and top with the second crust.

5   Cut small slits in the top crust for the steam to escape. If you like, brush the top of the pie with an egg wash and sprinkle with sanding sugar or granulated sugar. Want to add a cutout flower or leaf? Make them out of a scrap of dough and place on the egg-washed top before you add the sugar!

6   Bake for 40 to 45 minutes, or until the crust is golden brown and the filling is bubbling.

PECAN PIE

INGREDIENTS

½ BATCH BUTTER CRUST PIE DOUGH (PAGE 109)

6 TABLESPOONS BUTTER

1 CUP PACKED BROWN SUGAR

½ TEASPOON SALT

3 EGGS

¾ CUP CORN SYRUP

1 TABLESPOON VANILLA EXTRACT

2 CUPS PECANS

Pecan pie is a fall favorite. Our customers think pecan pie is perfect for either a late afternoon snack or a crowd-pleasing dessert to bring home for holiday dinners.

Makes one 9-inch pie

1   Roll out the pie dough and place the crust in the pie pan.

2   Preheat the oven to 350°F.

3   Melt the butter in a medium saucepan over low heat. Take off the heat and stir in the sugar and salt. Whisk in the eggs. Stir in the corn syrup and vanilla. Stir in the pecans. Pour the filling into the pie shell.

4   Bake for 40 to 50 minutes, or until the filling is set and a toothpick comes out clean (the pie will continue setting when you leave it out to cool on a wire rack).

TREATS ARE GOOD! TREATS ARE GOOD! TREATS ARE GOOD! TREATS ARE GOOD! TREATS ARE GOOD! TREATS ARE GOOD! TREATS ARE GOOD! TREATS ARE GOOD! TREATS ARE GOOD! TRE
RE GOOD! TREATS ARE GOOD! TREATS ARE GOOD! TREATS ARE GOOD! TREATS ARE GOOD! TREATS ARE GOOD! TREATS ARE GOOD! TREATS ARE GOOD! TREATS ARE GOOD! TREATS ARE G
TREATS ARE GOOD! TREATS ARE GOOD! TREATS ARE GOOD! TREATS ARE GOOD! TREATS ARE GOOD! TREATS ARE GOOD! TREATS ARE GOOD! TREATS ARE GOOD! TREATS ARE GOOD! TREA
RE GOOD! TREATS ARE GOOD! TREATS ARE GOOD! TREATS ARE GOOD! TREATS ARE GOOD! TREATS ARE GOOD! TREATS ARE GOOD! TREATS ARE GOOD! TREATS ARE GOOD! TREATS ARE GO

PUMPKIN PIE

INGREDIENTS

½ BATCH BUTTER
CRUST PIE DOUGH
(PAGE 108)

¾ CUP SUGAR

½ TEASPOON SALT

1 TEASPOON
GROUND CINNAMON

¼ TEASPOON
GROUND CLOVES

½ TEASPOON
GROUND GINGER

1 CAN (15 OUNCES)
PUMPKIN PUREE

2 EGGS

1 CAN (12 OUNCES)
EVAPORATED MILK

We make a lot of pumpkin pies each fall. They're not just for Thanksgiving, oh my, no!

Any crisp autumn afternoon is a fine time for a slice or a little Jr. pumpkin pie (so portable, just like a cupcake!).

Makes one 9-inch pie or 10 to 15 Jr. Pies

1   Roll out the pie dough and place the crust in the pie pan.

2   Preheat the oven to 350°F.

3   In a large bowl, combine the sugar, salt, cinnamon, cloves, and ginger. Add the pumpkin puree and mix well. Mix in the eggs. Stir in the evaporated milk. Pour the mixture into the piecrust.

4   Bake for 45 to 60 minutes (25 to 35 for Jr. Pies; see page 114), or until the crust is golden brown and a knife inserted into the pumpkin filling comes out clean.

MIXED BERRY PIE

INGREDIENTS

1 BATCH BUTTER CRUST PIE DOUGH (PAGE 109)

4 TO 5 CUPS MIXED BERRIES (A COMBINATION OF RASPBERRIES, BLACKBERRIES, BLUEBERRIES, AND STRAWBERRIES), FRESH OR FROZEN

¾ TO 1 CUP SUGAR, TO YOUR TASTE

2 TEASPOONS LEMON JUICE, OPTIONAL

¼ CUP FLOUR, PLUS 2 TABLESPOONS AS NEEDED

2 TABLESPOONS BUTTER

The great thing about a berry pie is that you can use either fresh or frozen berries, making it a year-round treat. Berry pie à la mode is oh so delish. I like to make berry pies either with a full top crust or with more of an open top with strips of crust across the top (you can make a fancy lattice top or just layer strips across or add spiral strips—create a top of your own design!).

Makes one 9-inch pie

1 Preheat the oven to 350°F.

2 If you're using frozen berries, allow time for the berries to thaw and drain.

3 Roll out the pie dough and place the bottom crust in the pie pan. In a large bowl, mix the berries, sugar, and lemon juice, if desired. Sprinkle in the flour and mix, adding a bit more if you need to depending on the amount of berries, how juicy they are, and your personal preference (I don't mind a little bit of a runny, juicy pie, but some prefer a firmer filling). Pour the berries into the piecrust and dot the filling with butter.

4 Add the top crust and make slits for the steam to escape.

5 Bake for 30 to 40 minutes, or until the crust is golden brown and the filling is bubbling.

STRAWBERRY PIE

²/₃ CUP FRUIT JAM
(RASPBERRY IS MY
FAVE, BUT APRICOT
OR STRAWBERRY
WORKS, TOO—ADD A
TEASPOON OF FRESH
LEMON JUICE IF
USING STRAWBERRY)

5 CUPS
STRAWBERRIES,
HALVED (OR ANY
MIX OF BERRIES YOU
CHOOSE)

1 BATCH BUTTER
CRUST (PAGE 109,
BLIND BAKED),
GRAHAM CRACKER
CRUST (PAGE 112),
OR SHORTBREAD
CRUST (PAGE 113)

WHIPPED CREAM
(PAGE 74) FOR
SERVING, OPTIONAL

This pie is my nod to an old-fashioned fresh strawberry pie. It has a lighter glaze, which I prefer, but still has the lovely mix of fresh berries and crust. In addition to using strawberries, you can mix in other fresh berries if you wish.

Makes one 9-inch pie

1   In a small saucepan over low heat, melt the jam (this will happen quickly). Pour the jam over the berries in a large bowl and toss to coat.

2   Pour the berries into the piecrust. If you want to arrange the berries after putting them in the crust, use your fingers to make adjustments. No one will see! Drizzle any leftover jam over the berries. If you want a fancier presentation, arrange the strawberries in the crust without tossing them in the jam and coat them with the jam using a pastry brush.

3   Chill until ready to serve. Serve with whipped cream, if you like. This pie is best served the day it's made, but leftovers the next day are nothing to sneeze at.

PEACH PIE

INGREDIENTS

1 BATCH BUTTER
CRUST PIE DOUGH
(PAGE 109)

5 TO 6 CUPS PEELED
AND SLICED FRESH
PEACHES (SEE TIP)

1 TEASPOON
LEMON JUICE

½ CUP DARK
BROWN SUGAR,
OR AS DESIRED

¼ CUP SUGAR

¼ TEASPOON
GROUND CINNAMON,
NUTMEG, OR
CARDAMOM,
OPTIONAL

¼ TEASPOON
VANILLA EXTRACT,
OPTIONAL

3 TABLESPOONS
CORNSTARCH,
POTATO STARCH,
OR FLOUR

3 TABLESPOONS
BUTTER

Peach pie is such a happy pie. Maybe because peaches are in season during the summer, peach pie seems to call out for taking it easy and enjoying the day.

Makes one 9-inch pie

1   Preheat the oven to 350°F.

2   Roll out the pie dough and place the bottom crust in the pie pan. In a large bowl, toss the peaches with the lemon juice and sugars. Add the spices and vanilla, as desired. Add the thickener of your choice and stir to coat the peaches. Pour the peaches into the piecrust. Dot with butter.

3   Add the top crust and make slits for the steam to escape.

4   Bake for 35 to 45 minutes, or until the crust is golden brown and the filling is bubbling.

VARIATION: MAKE AN OPEN-FACED PEACH PIE WITH A SHORTBREAD CRUST (PAGE 113), EITHER BAKED AS ABOVE OR AS A FRESH FRUIT PIE FOLLOWING THE STRAWBERRY PIE RECIPE (PAGE 119).

TIP: YOU CAN PEEL THE PEACHES AS THEY ARE, OR BLANCH THEM IN HOT WATER FOR 30 TO 40 SECONDS, THEN PUT THEM IN A BOWL OF COLD WATER TO COOL BEFORE PEELING.

LEMON MERINGUE PIE

Some people love a good old-fashioned lemon meringue pie. Some love it even better without the meringue with just whipped cream on top. Some people (me) absolutely love both. Feel free to make the pie with or without!

1 BATCH BUTTER
CRUST PIE DOUGH
(PAGE 109)

1 CUP SUGAR

2 TABLESPOONS
FLOUR

3 TABLESPOONS
CORNSTARCH

¼ TEASPOON SALT

1½ CUPS WATER

JUICE AND ZEST OF
2 LEMONS (ABOUT
⅓ CUP JUICE)

4 EGG YOLKS,
BEATEN

2 TABLESPOONS
BUTTER

4 EGG WHITES

6 TABLESPOONS
SUGAR

Makes one 9-inch pie

1   Preheat the oven to 425°F and blind bake the piecrust (see page 108). Set aside.

2   Lower the heat to 350°F.

3   In a medium saucepan, whisk the sugar, flour, cornstarch, and salt. Whisk in a small amount of water to form a paste and prevent lumps. Whisk in the remaining water, the lemon juice, and zest.

4   Cook over medium-high heat, stirring often, until the mixture comes to a boil. Boil for 1 minute. Remove the pan from the heat.

5   In a medium bowl, whisk the egg yolks. As you whisk vigorously, gradually add ½ cup of the hot sugar mixture. Return the pan to medium heat and, again whisking vigorously, add the egg mixture to the pan again. Whisk constantly until the mixture returns to a boil, then whisk in the butter and continue whisking until the mixture thickens, 1 or 2 minutes. Pour the hot liquid into the piecrust.

6   To make the meringue, in a large clean bowl, beat the egg whites, gradually adding the sugar and beating until stiff peaks form. Immediately spread the meringue over the pie, all the way to the edges of the crust. Bake for 10 to 12 minutes, until the meringue is tinged golden. Allow the pie to sit at room temperature for 2 to 3 hours, then refrigerate for 3 to 4 hours, uncovered.

VARIATION: IF YOU PREFER, YOU CAN FORGO THE MERINGUE AND USE SWEETENED WHIPPED CREAM (PAGE 74) ON TOP. Spread a layer of whipped cream over the top of the cooled pie and chill until ready to serve, or leave the pie plain and garnish each slice with whipped cream as you serve.

VANILLA CREAM PIE

INGREDIENTS

1 BATCH BUTTER
CRUST (PAGE 109),
GRAHAM CRACKER
CRUST (PAGE 112),
DOUBLE CHOCOLATE
CRUST (PAGE 111),
OR GINGERSNAP
CRUST (PAGE 112)

1¼ CUPS MILK

1¼ CUPS HEAVY
CREAM

⅓ CUP PLUS
2 TABLESPOONS
SUGAR

PINCH SALT

2 EGGS, SLIGHTLY
BEATEN

3 EGG YOLKS

¼ CUP PLUS
1 TABLESPOON
CORNSTARCH

2 TABLESPOONS
BUTTER

2 TEASPOONS
VANILLA EXTRACT

WHIPPED CREAM
(PAGE 74) FOR
SERVING, OPTIONAL

Vanilla cream pie, vanilla cream pie, la la, la, la la, la, vanilla cream pie. Old-fashioned and supersatisfying, vanilla cream pie is worth singing about. It's also the basic cream pie that's easily transformed into banana cream pie.

Makes one 9-inch pie

1   Preheat the oven to 350°F and blind bake the piecrust (see page 108).

2   In a medium saucepan over medium heat, heat the milk and cream. As the mixture becomes hot, add ⅓ cup sugar and the salt and bring the mixture to a near boil. Take off the heat.

3   In a bowl, mix the eggs, egg yolks, cornstarch, and remaining 2 tablespoons sugar until smooth. Whisk a little of the hot milk mixture into the egg mixture, add a bit more hot milk mixture, whisking vigorously, then whisk all the egg mixture into the milk mixture.

4   Return the saucepan to medium heat. Stirring continuously, cook for about 2 minutes, or until the mixture thickens to a puddinglike consistency, then remove from the heat.

5   Pour the mixture into a mixing bowl. Add the butter and vanilla and whisk or mix with an electric mixer for 15 to 20 minutes, or until the mixture has fully thickened.

6   Pour the filling into the piecrust. Refrigerate until ready to serve.

7   Top with whipped cream, if you'd like!

TREATS ARE GOOD! TREATS ARE GOOD! TREATS ARE GOOD! TREATS ARE GOOD! TREATS ARE GOOD! TREATS ARE GOOD! TREATS ARE GOOD! TREATS ARE GOOD! TREATS ARE GOOD! TRE.
RE GOOD! TREATS ARE GOOD! TREATS ARE GOOD! TREATS ARE GOOD! TREATS ARE GOOD! TREATS ARE GOOD! TREATS ARE GOOD! TREATS ARE GOOD! TREATS ARE G
TREATS ARE GOOD! TREATS ARE GOOD! TREATS ARE GOOD! TREATS ARE GOOD! TREATS ARE GOOD! TREATS ARE GOOD! TREATS ARE GOOD! TREATS ARE GOOD! TREA
RE GOOD! TREATS ARE GOOD! TREATS ARE GOOD! TREATS ARE GOOD! TREATS ARE GOOD! TREATS ARE GOOD! TREATS ARE GOOD! TREATS ARE GOOD! TREATS ARE GOOD! TREATS ARE GOOD! TREATS ARE GOOD! TREATS ARE GOOD! TREATS ARE GOOD!

BANANA CREAM PIE

INGREDIENTS

VANILLA CREAM PIE
FILLING (PAGE 122)

1 BAKED GRAHAM
CRACKER CRUST
(PAGE 112) OR BLIND
BAKED BUTTER
CRUST (PAGE 109)

3 OR 4 RIPE
BANANAS, THINLY
SLICED

WHIPPED CREAM
(PAGE 74) FOR
SERVING, OPTIONAL

Add some fresh ripe bananas to a vanilla cream pie and you've got yourself one fine banana cream pie!

Makes one 9-inch pie

Spread half the vanilla cream filling in the pie shell. Lay the banana slices in a single layer on top of the filling. Pour the rest of the vanilla filling over the bananas. Chill until ready to serve. Garnish with whipped cream, if you like.

VARIATION: TRY THE DOUBLE CHOCOLATE COOKIE CRUST (PAGE 111) WITH YOUR BANANA CREAM PIE!

Top with whipped cream and garnish with some shaved chocolate.

CHOCOLATE PIE

INGREDIENTS

¾ CUP SEMISWEET
CHOCOLATE CHIPS

¼ CUP MILK

1 TEASPOON
VANILLA EXTRACT

⅛ TEASPOON SALT

1 CUP HEAVY
WHIPPING CREAM

1 BLIND BAKED
CLASSIC CHOCOLATE
COOKIE CRUST
(PAGE 110)

This is a staff favorite. It's not a traditional chocolate cream pie but more of a chocolate whipped cream dream of a pie!

Makes one 9-inch pie

1   Melt the chocolate in a double boiler or small saucepan.

2   In another small saucepan, heat the milk over low heat until it is very warm but not boiling.

3   Add the hot milk, vanilla, and salt to the melted chocolate and mix well. Refrigerate the mixture until cooled.

4   Before you whip the cream, make sure the bowl is very clean. Put the bowl and paddle or whisk in the refrigerator or freezer for at least 15 minutes before you begin. In your chilled bowl or mixer bowl, whip the cream just until stiff peaks form. With a spatula, fold in the cool chocolate mixture into the whipped cream and pour it into the piecrust.

5   Chill for 2 to 4 hours before serving. Garnish with shaved chocolate or chocolate sprinkles as you wish.

6   Invite all your most fanatic chocolate lovers over and dig in.

Cake or Pie?
The Age-Old Question . . .

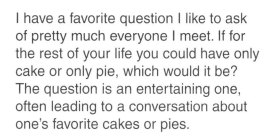

I have a favorite question I like to ask of pretty much everyone I meet. If for the rest of your life you could have only cake or only pie, which would it be? The question is an entertaining one, often leading to a conversation about one's favorite cakes or pies.

Now, most people know the answer without even thinking. The word *cake* or *pie* comes flying out of their mouths before they can even blink. I actually think the world *is* divided between those who'd choose cake and those who'd choose pie.

Though occasionally, I do meet someone who struggles with the question.

I can only watch the internal struggle for a moment or two before reassuring them. "But isn't it lucky that's not the way the world works? You don't actually have to choose." Whew!

Cake or pie? I must admit, I, too, have a very clear idea of which I'd choose but luckily I can have my cake and eat pie, too.

I am truly a fan of both.

SPECIALS

('THOUGH ALL TREATS ARE SPECIAL . . .)

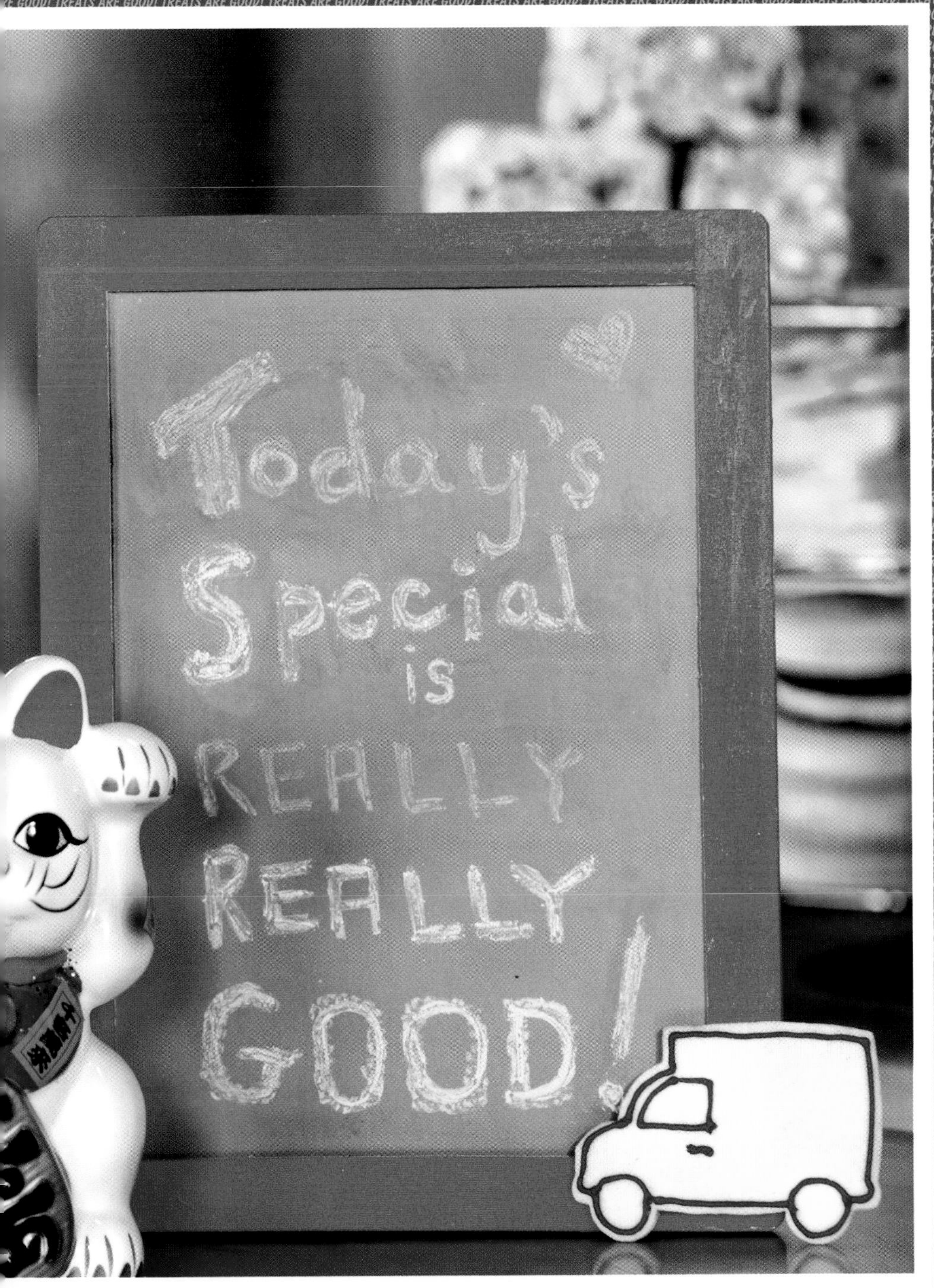
Today's
Special
is
REALLY
REALLY
GOOD!

I like to feature daily Specials on the truck and at The Truck Stop.

Seasonal and holiday Specials are always fun to look forward to, but every day deserves something special. Some Specials start out as houseguests and end up moving in to stay. Some Specials pop up only once in a while upon request. And some Specials have been inspired by a customer.

One customer in particular likes to stop by each Wednesday with a suggestion for the next Special he'd like to see. They always involve coconut. Always. You'll see . . .

And sometimes we have contests. One contest was to name our chocolate sandwich cookie, which really didn't have much of a name. I had decided that it needed a better name than *that chocolate sandwich cookie thingy.* The winning entry was the Chocolate Trucker. We can't imagine not having Truckers on the menu now! Another contest was to come up with the best name (but no recipe) for a new Special. One of the winners from that contest is also in this chapter.

You can do the same at home, if you'd like. Ask your spouse, date, friends, or kids to come up with an idea for a Special, either by ingredients or just by name, and see what you dream up!

CUSTOMER SPECIALS

With both of the following customer-inspired recipes, you can make a whole batch or just a few cookies, since they're both based on basic cookie dough recipes. You may wish to make some the usual way and some as Specials!

THE NUTTY COWORKER

INGREDIENTS

OATMEAL COOKIE DOUGH (PAGE 10)

NUTS (PECANS, WALNUTS, PEANUTS, ALMONDS, ANY MIX YOU LIKE, SALTED OR UNSALTED)

RAISINS OR CHOCOLATE CHIPS, OPTIONAL

We had a contest to come up with a great name for a Special without a recipe attached. That way, I could create a treat based on the winning name. We chose a few winning names, and one of them was the Nutty Coworker.

Some nutty coworkers are just a little nutty and others are totally nuts. Add about ⅓ cup mixed nuts and raisins to 1 cup cookie dough, more or less if you please—you know your nutty coworker better than I! And are there chocolate chips involved?

TREATS ARE GOOD! TREATS ARE GOOD! TREATS ARE GOOD! TREATS ARE GOOD! TREATS ARE GOOD! TREATS ARE GOOD! TREATS ARE GOOD! TREATS ARE GOOD! TREATS ARE GOOD! TREATS ARE GOOD! TRE.
RE GOOD! TREATS ARE GOOD! TREATS ARE GOOD! TREATS ARE GOOD! TREATS ARE GOOD! TREATS ARE GOOD! TREATS ARE GOOD! TREATS ARE GOOD! TREATS ARE GOOD! TREATS ARE G
TREATS ARE GOOD! TREATS ARE GOOD! TREATS ARE GOOD! TREATS ARE GOOD! TREATS ARE GOOD! TREATS ARE GOOD! TREATS ARE GOOD! TREATS ARE GOOD! TREATS ARE GOOD! TREA
E GOOD! TREATS ARE GOOD! TREATS ARE GOOD! TREATS ARE GOOD! TREATS ARE GOOD! TREATS ARE GOOD! TREATS ARE GOOD! TREATS ARE GOOD! TREATS ARE GOOD! TREATS ARE GO

THE COCONUT MITCH

INGREDIENTS

CHOCOLATE CHIPPER
DOUGH (PAGE 4)

SHREDDED
SWEETENED
COCONUT

This Special was made at the request of one of our customers in Midtown Manhattan. He kept asking for a chocolate chip cookie with coconut. Being a regular and a really lovely man, he gently reminded me of his request every week for months. *You got the coconut chocolate chip yet?* he'd say with a smile. One day, he got the surprise of his life—I'd made coconut chocolate chip cookies just for him. *Put it in big letters on the menu*, he urged. *The customers are gonna love it!*

What's your name? I asked. He'd been coming to the truck for a very long time, and the least I could do was name the cookie after him! To this day, even people who don't know him are happy to see the Coconut Mitch on the menu. It's good. Just ask Mitch.

Mix 1 cup dough with ⅓ cup coconut, scoop out your cookies, and bake as usual. And remember, a man named Mitch in Midtown Manhattan is smiling just knowing you are out there somewhere baking his favorite cookie.

DESSERT NACHOS

INGREDIENTS

CARAMEL CREME
COOKIE DOUGH
(PAGE 24)

CHOCOLATE COOKIE
DOUGH (PAGE 12)

1 TO 3 CHOCOLATE
CHIP BROWNIES
(PAGE 40), CHOPPED
INTO SMALL CUBES

1 TO 3 PECAN
BUTTERSCOTCH
BARS (PAGE 48),
CHOPPED INTO
SMALL CUBES

1 TO 3 CLASSIC RICE
CRISPY SQUARES
(PAGE 50), CHOPPED
INTO SMALL CUBES

HOT FUDGE TOPPING
(PAGE 71) OR
CHOCOLATE SAUCE

WHIPPED CREAM
(PAGE 74)

CONFETTI SPRINKLES
(OR SPRINKLES OF
YOUR CHOOSING)

CHOCOLATE JIMMIES
OR NUTS, OPTIONAL

SPECIAL EQUIPMENT:
PAPER NACHO BOATS
(OR ANY SERVING
BOWL HANDY)

One time for an event, I was asked to come up with an over-the-top off-the-menu item. This is what I came up with—and now we get a lot of requests for it! What are dessert nachos, you ask? They're the cookie version of regular nachos, with cookies that look like chips, topped with chopped-up treats, chocolate sauce, whipped cream, and sprinkles. They're crazy—and crazy good.

1   Preheat the oven to 325°F.

2   Roll out enough cookie dough for the amount of chips you'd like to make. Cut out triangles the size of tortilla chips. Place the triangles on 2 baking sheets, one for each kind of dough. Place some of the cookies going up the edge of the pan so that they will bake in curled or bent positions. With some flat "chips" and some curled or bent, they really do resemble tortilla chips!

3   Bake the chocolate cookies for 9 to 11 minutes and the caramel cremes 10 to 12 minutes. Cool on the baking sheets.

4   Now it's time to get your beans and guacamole ready! Cut the brownies, pecan butterscotch bars, and rice crispy squares into small cubes.

5   Salsa next! Make your hot fudge topping and whipped cream, or get out the store-bought ready-to-go versions. If you happen to have paper nacho boats, wow, fantastic! Otherwise, bring out your best nacho bowl or platter.

6   Place a layer of chips first. Then add all the chopped ingredients on top and in between the chips. Add some hot fudge topping or chocolate sauce. Dollop whipped cream across the top. Add more topping. Sprinkle with confetti sprinkles, jimmies, or nuts. And that, my baker friends, is dessert nachos.

SPRINKLES

+

CHOCOLATE SAUCE

+

WHIPPED CREAM

+

BROWNIE & CRISPY SQUARES

+

COOKIE CHIPS

CAKE SANDWICHES

Yes, you heard right, cake sandwiches. A few years ago, I decided I wanted to make peanut-butter-and-jelly cake sandwiches for a party. I really wanted it to look like a PB&J sandwich, so I sliced some cake to look like slices of bread to make a sandwich. I cut the "bread" slices about 2 by 3 or 3 by 3 inches, and then cut them into triangles. Feel free to make them bigger if you'd like!

This is a fun way to serve cake, especially when you don't want to bother with utensils. My two favorites are the PB&J cake sandwich and the frosting sandwich—simply cake slices with frosting in between. Easy to pick up, and just the right size. And it's kind of fun to say, "I'm eating a frosting sandwich."

FOR THE PB&J,
I use straight-up peanut butter and jam, as I would in a sandwich, with vanilla cake.

FOR THE FROSTING SANDWICH,
use the cake and frosting of your choice. Vanilla cake seems to hold together better than chocolate cake, so for chocolate cake sandwiches, put each sandwich in a cupcake paper for easy eating. Coconut cake or lemon cake would work well, too!

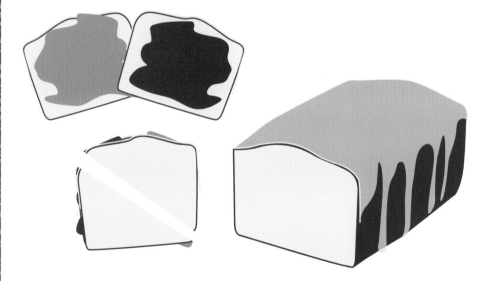

138 • THE TREATS TRUCK BAKING BOOK

TREATS ARE GOOD! TREATS ARE GOOD! TREATS ARE GOOD! TREATS ARE GOOD! TREATS ARE GOOD! TREATS ARE GOOD! TREATS ARE GOOD! TREATS ARE GOOD! TREATS ARE GOOD! TRE
RE GOOD! TREATS ARE GOOD! TREATS ARE GOOD! TREATS ARE GOOD! TREATS ARE GOOD! TREATS ARE GOOD! TREATS ARE GOOD! TREATS ARE GOOD! TREATS ARE GOOD! TREATS ARE G
TREATS ARE GOOD! TREATS ARE GOOD! TREATS ARE GOOD! TREATS ARE GOOD! TREATS ARE GOOD! TREATS ARE GOOD! TREATS ARE GOOD! TREATS ARE GOOD! TREATS ARE GOOD! TREA
E GOOD! TREATS ARE GOOD! TREATS ARE GOOD! TREATS ARE GOOD! TREATS ARE GOOD! TREATS ARE GOOD! TREATS ARE GOOD! TREATS ARE GOOD! TREATS ARE GOOD! TREATS ARE GO

BROWNIE SUNDAES

INGREDIENTS

BROWNIE OR BAR (PECAN BUTTERSCOTCH, ANYONE? SEE PAGE 48)

ICE CREAM

BANANA OR BERRIES

INSTANT ESPRESSO POWDER

CARAMEL TOPPING

HOT FUDGE TOPPING

JAM

WHIPPED CREAM

CHOPPED NUTS

SHAVED OR CHOPPED CHOCOLATE

SPRINKLES

Play home ice cream parlor and whip up a big sundae that's sure to please. A big sundae with a big spoon! Sometimes for dinner parties, I like to make little Jr. Sundaes, too. Fun, and just the right size. Set out bowls of the toppings so everyone can create their own!

Makes as many as you like!

1   Take your favorite brownie or bar. If you want, warm it a bit in the oven or toaster oven or give it a very quick shot in a microwave oven. Put the brownie in a bowl.

2   Add a scoop or two of your favorite ice cream. Add a sliced banana or berries, or if you're a coffee fan, sprinkle a little espresso powder over the ice cream. Top with caramel or hot fudge topping or both. Like jam? A little jam is nice, too.

3   Add whipped cream and nuts, shaved or chopped chocolate, and sprinkles for the smile factor. Take a spoon and dive in!

STRAWBERRY SHORTCAKE

INGREDIENTS

3 CUPS FLOUR

3 TABLESPOONS PLUS ¼ CUP SUGAR

1½ TEASPOONS BAKING POWDER

¾ TEASPOON SALT

12 TABLESPOONS COLD BUTTER, CUT INTO SMALL PIECES

1½ CUPS HEAVY CREAM

1½ TEASPOONS VANILLA EXTRACT

3 PINTS STRAWBERRIES, HULLED AND SLICED

WHIPPED CREAM (PAGE 74)

Light and lovely! When someone sets a plate of shortcake and berries and whipped cream in front of you, it really must be a good day.

Makes 9 shortcakes

1   Preheat the oven to 375°F.

2   In a large bowl, combine the flour, 3 tablespoons sugar, baking powder, and salt. Use a fork to cut in the butter until the mixture resembles coarse crumbs. Add the cream and vanilla and mix with a fork. Gently knead by hand, but do not overmix. Cover and chill for 20 minutes.

3   Pat and shape the dough on a floured surface into a square about 8 inches wide. Cut it into 9 biscuits. Place the biscuits on a parchment-lined or greased pan. Bake for 18 to 20 minutes, or until golden.

4   To prepare the strawberries, mix the sliced berries and the ¼ cup sugar in a bowl. Set aside for at least 20 minutes to get nice and syrupy.

5   To serve, slice a piece of shortcake in half, layer with the strawberries, and add a dollop of whipped cream!

VARIATION: YOU CAN ALSO USE JUICY FRESH PEACHES, NECTARINES, OR MIXED BERRIES!

AMAZING CAKE

Okay, this recipe is top secret, so make sure no one is looking over your shoulder right now. Ready? I'll share this recipe with you if you promise to pass it on only to your closest friends and relatives, and they must also promise to keep it a secret. Agreed?

So here's the deal. Come up with a cake idea you really love, maybe with a theme or inspiration. Choose the kind of cake to bake and pick the right frostings, filling, and additions to finish your creation. Call it Amazing Cake.

One of my best friends Leslie Louise Newton and I love coming up with Amazing Cakes. Some of our favorites? A movie snacks cake, a banana split cake, a trick-or-treat cake for Halloween.

Whatever you create, it's yours, so call it Amazing Cake. You might just start a family tradition. You may get requests from your friends for new and amazing creations. You can take requests or simply dream up what makes you smile. And, that, my fellow amazing bakers, is Amazing Cake.

MOVIE SNACKS CAKE

A two-layer vanilla cake with buttercream frosting in the middle, studded with Junior Mints, Raisinets, and Milk Duds. Frost the cake with buttercream frosting and decorate the top and sides with popcorn. Add red licorice vines on top.

BANANA SPLIT CAKE

A two-layer vanilla cake (or one layer vanilla, one chocolate) with sliced bananas and chocolate filling in the middle and topped with lots of whipped cream, hot fudge, nuts, and maraschino cherries.

TRICK-OR-TREAT CAKE

A vanilla cake with M&Ms and chopped-up candy bars baked inside. Frost the cake with buttercream frosting and stud it with candy corn, M&Ms, and all your favorite Halloween candy.

ICE CREAM SANDWICHES

Ice cream sandwiches are quite delightful and delish—and supereasy to assemble out of cookies and brownies.

Mix&Match all kinds of combinations of cookies, bars, and ice cream flavors—you decide!

Chocolate chip cookies!

Chocolate cookies!

Sugar cookies!

Peanut butter cookies!

Oatmeal cookies!

Brownies!

Pecan butterscotch bars!

Chocolate chocolate chippers!

1 Here we go. Get the ice cream of your choice and scoop it onto

• your favorite cookie. Top with a second cookie.

• a brownie or butterscotch bar. Slice the bar in half, put a scoop of ice cream on one half, and top with the other.

2 Roll the edges of your ice cream sandwiches in sprinkles or chocolate shavings or jimmies, if you please.

3 Wrap each sandwich in plastic wrap and stick in the freezer. Let them set for at least ½ hour. That's it.

4 Take them out. Eat right away. Do a dance of appreciation.

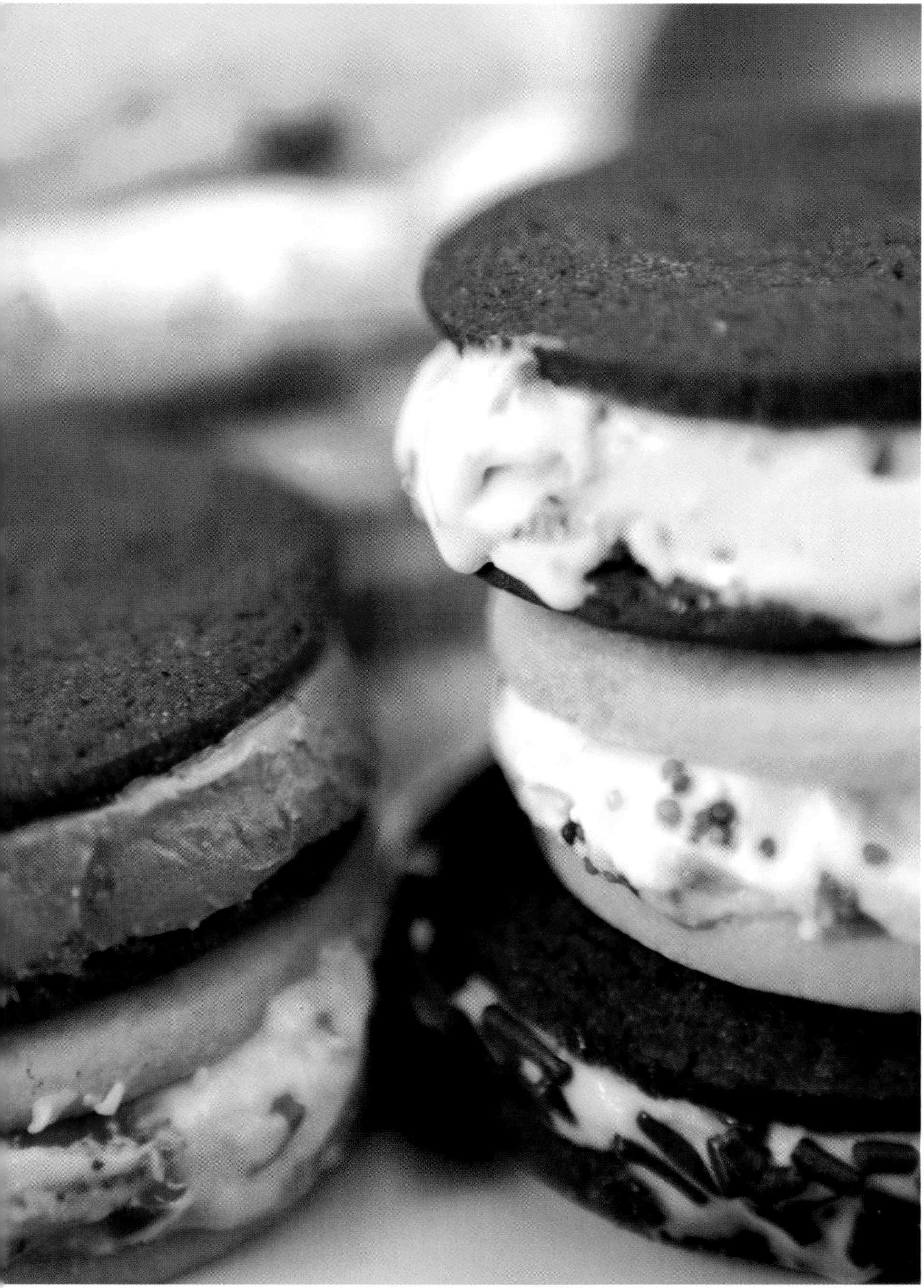

ICE CREAM PIE

INGREDIENTS

FAVORITE PIECRUST
(PAGES 108 TO 113)

FAVORITE ICE
CREAM, SOFTENED

CHOPPED NUTS OR
CANDY OR CRUSHED
SUGAR CONES, AS
YOU WISH

CHOCOLATE SAUCE
OR HOT FUDGE
TOPPING (PAGE 71),
OPTIONAL, BUT
COME ON . . .

CARAMEL SAUCE

WHIPPED CREAM—
I THINK YES

A cookie crust filled with ice cream? What's not to love about that?

Makes one 9-inch pie

1   Fill your favorite cookie crust with your favorite ice cream and freeze it for at least 1 hour. (If you like, make a layer of one flavor, freeze it for 30 minutes, add a second layer of another flavor.) Sprinkle chopped nuts or candy or crushed cones in between the layers, if you wish. (Freeze until ready to serve.)

2   Top with chocolate sauce, or caramel sauce or whipped cream. And sprinkles are always welcome.

TREATS ARE GOOD! TREATS ARE GOOD! TREATS ARE GOOD! TREATS ARE GOOD! TREATS ARE GOOD! TREATS ARE GOOD! TREATS ARE GOOD! TREATS ARE GOOD! TREATS ARE GOOD! TRE.
ARE GOOD! TREATS ARE GOOD! TREATS ARE GOOD! TREATS ARE GOOD! TREATS ARE GOOD! TREATS ARE GOOD! TREATS ARE GOOD! TREATS ARE GOOD! TREATS ARE GOOD! TREATS ARE GOOD! TREA
TREATS ARE GOOD! TREATS ARE GOOD! TREATS ARE GOOD! TREATS ARE GOOD! TREATS ARE GOOD! TREATS ARE GOOD! TREATS ARE GOOD! TREATS ARE GOOD! TREATS ARE GOOD! TREA
E GOOD! TREATS ARE GOOD! TREATS ARE GOOD! TREATS ARE GOOD! TREATS ARE GOOD! TREATS ARE GOOD! TREATS ARE GOOD! TREATS ARE GOOD! TREATS ARE GOOD! TREATS ARE GO

ICE CREAM CAKE

INGREDIENTS

ONE 9-INCH
ROUND CAKE

4 PINTS (½ GALLON)
TO 1 GALLON ICE
CREAM, SOFTENED

OPTIONAL FILLINGS:
COARSE COOKIE
CRUMBS, BROWNIE
SLICES, CRUSHED
SUGAR CONES, OR
NUTS

HOT FUDGE SAUCE,
CARAMEL SAUCE, OR
WHIPPED CREAM,
FOR SERVING

An ice cream cake is fun for birthdays or special occasions, especially if you know you'll have ice cream people at the table.

CAKE / *Ice Cream* / CAKE

1 Using a serrated knife, slice the cake through the middle horizontally, as if you were slicing a roll to make a sandwich. Wrap each half in plastic wrap and freeze until ready to assemble the cake.

2 Lay a plate on a large piece of plastic wrap and lay one cake half on the plate. Add a thick layer of softened ice cream to the top of the cake. Add the top layer of cake and then wrap the plastic wrap around the whole thing and stick it in the freezer for 1 hour or longer. It will look super just as it is, kind of like a big sandwich cookie, but you can also frost the cake all over with softened ice cream.

OPTIONAL: Add a layer of cookie pieces, crushed sugar cones, or anything you'd like before placing the top layer of cake.

Ice Cream / CAKE / *Ice Cream*

1 In a springform pan, place one layer of softened ice cream. Add a layer of cake, cookie crumbs, or thinly sliced brownies on top of the ice cream layer. (The cake can be the same size as the pan, or cut it to fit.) Add a thick layer of ice cream on top.

2 Freeze for 1 hour or longer. Take it out and release it from the springform pan.

3 Serve with hot fudge sauce or caramel sauce and whipped cream on top.

VARIATION: ADD A LAYER OF COOKIE CRUMBS, THINLY SLICED BROWNIES, OR OTHER ADD-INS IN BETWEEN ONE OF THE LAYERS IN PLACE OF OR IN ADDITION TO THE CAKE.

TREATS ARE GOOD! TREATS ARE GOOD! TREATS ARE GOOD! TREATS ARE GOOD! TREATS ARE GOOD! TREATS ARE GOOD! TREATS ARE GOOD! TREATS ARE GOOD! TREATS ARE GOOD! TREAT.
E GOOD! TREATS ARE GOOD! TREATS ARE GOOD! TREATS ARE GOOD! TREATS ARE GOOD! TREATS ARE GOOD! TREATS ARE GOOD! TREATS ARE GOOD! TREATS ARE GOOD! TREATS ARE GOOD! TREATS ARE GOOD! TREA
REATS ARE GOOD! TREATS ARE GOOD! TREATS ARE GOOD! TREATS ARE GOOD! TREATS ARE GOOD! TREATS ARE GOOD! TREATS ARE GOOD! TREATS ARE GOOD! TREATS ARE GOOD! TREA

HOT CHOCOLATE & MEXICAN HOT CHOCOLATE

I love hot chocolate. Sometimes a classic chocolate totally hits the spot and sometimes a Mexican chocolate is what I really want. Here are the basic recipes to start, and then see if you want to add more chocolate or sugar or cream until you get your perfect tailor-made mix.

In the summertime, it's also great to make iced hot chocolate! Just let it cool and keep in the fridge. Pour over ice when serving. Add some iced coffee to make it a mocha.

Classic iced chocolate and Mexican iced chocolate are both really good!

HOT CHOCOLATE

INGREDIENTS

Makes 2 servings

2 CUPS MILK

½ CUP HALF-AND-HALF

1 TABLESPOON COCOA POWDER

⅓ CUP CHOPPED SEMISWEET CHOCOLATE OR CHOCOLATE CHIPS

1 TO 2 TABLESPOONS SUGAR, DEPENDING ON HOW SWEET YOU LIKE IT

WHIPPED CREAM (PAGE 74) OR MARSHMALLOWS, FOR SERVING

1. Over medium heat, warm the milk in a small saucepan.

2. Whisk in the half-and-half and cocoa powder. Add the chocolate and sugar and froth with the whisk until the chocolate is melted and the milk is hot. Take off the heat.

3. Pour into mugs and top with whipped cream or marshmallows.

VARIATION: MAKE IT A MOCHA—ADD FRESH HOT COFFEE, ESPRESSO, OR INSTANT ESPRESSO POWDER TO YOUR LIKING.

MEXICAN HOT CHOCOLATE

OD! TREAT
EATS ARE
OOD! TREA
TS ARE GC
OD! TREAT
EATS ARE
OOD! TREA
ATS ARE G
OD! TREAT
TS ARE GC
RE GOOD!
I TREATS
GOOD! TR
EATS ARE
E GOOD!
TS ARE GC
OOD! TREA
EATS ARE
ARE GOOL
GOOD! TR
EATS ARE
I TREATS
GOOD! TR
TS ARE GC
GOOD! TR
EATS ARE
OOD! TRE
RE GOOD!
I TREATS
TREATS A
E GOOD!
TS ARE G
I TREATS
REATS AR
E GOOD!
EATS ARE
I TREATS
EATS ARE
OOD! TRE
TS ARE G
I TREATS
ATS ARE
ARE GOO
TS ARE G
TREATS A
EATS ARE
E GOOD! T
I TREATS
GOOD! TR
EATS ARE
E GOOD!
TS ARE G
OD! TREA
EATS ARE
OD! TREA
TS ARE G
OOD! TREA
EATS ARE
RE GOOD!
S ARE GO
OOD! TRE
S ARE GO
RE GOOD!
ARE GOC
GOOD! TI
TREATS A
E GOOD!
EATS AR
OD! TREA
EATS ARE
GOOD! TI
TREATS A
OOD! TR
ATS ARE
GOOD! TR
REATS AR
OD! TREA
ARE GOC
GOOD! TI
EATS AR

INGREDIENTS

2 CUPS MILK

1 DISK MEXICAN
HOT CHOCOLATE
(SEE NOTE)

½ CUP HALF-
AND-HALF

1 TABLESPOON
COCOA POWDER

WHIPPED CREAM

Makes 2 servings

1   Over medium heat, warm the milk and Mexican hot
    chocolate disk in a small saucepan.

2   Whisk in the half-and-half and cocoa powder. Whisk until
    all the chocolate is melted and the milk is hot. Take off
    the heat.

3   Pour into mugs and top with whipped cream.

*Note: I buy Mexican hot chocolate at the grocery store;
the brands Ibarra or Abuelita are easy to find. If you can't
find it where you live, just make the regular hot chocolate
recipe and add a mixture of 2 teaspoons ground cinnamon
and 1 teaspoon vanilla. (Mixing them prevents clumping.)*

SNAPSHOTS
(OR, A DAY WITH THE TREATS TRUCK)

We have a lot of regulars. We know many of them not by name, but by the treats they like or their day of the week to come by the truck. There's Mr. One Oatmeal Chocolate Chipper and a Jammy and Ms. Wednesday Carrot Cake Center Slice. One little girl I think of as the Sugar Dot Girl comes with her mother for a little Sugar Dot to eat right away and another Dot in a bag. ("One for now, one for later!" her mother sings out to her, and she repeats it to me with a smile: "One for now, one for later!") Two other little girls and their mom on the Upper West Side stop by the truck on Thursdays (the Thursday family) and delight in picking out a special treat for each of them to take home for after dinner. They have many favorite choices, especially involving chocolate. A lot of workers in Midtown Manhattan bring lists of what to bring back to the office for all their office mates. And a certain mailman in Brooklyn stops by on Saturdays as he makes his rounds for a brownie or perhaps a cupcake and to wish us a good day.

We love our spots and all the customers in each neighborhood. I'm sure a lot of business owners are equally fond of their customers. It's a special thing, these moments to exchange a few words and a smile and a nibble from the sample tray. "Corner Brownies with nuts?" I ask the student on Eighteenth Street and Seventh Avenue on his way home from school. "Or something different this time?"

Our customers are truly the best in the world and the very best part of having The Treats Truck!

ABOUT US

The Treats Truck has many regular spots around New York City and also appears at special events and parties. Our truck, Sugar, is a used truck that we fixed up and made into our bake shop on wheels! He runs on compressed natural gas (CNG) like a lot of city buses. It's a greener type of fuel, but we like to think that he also runs on chocolate. And, yes, Sugar is a boy truck. We've been told that vehicles, like boats, are supposed to be female, but Sugar is a boy truck. He just is. He's the best.

The Treats Truck Stop is in Brooklyn. That's where we make all the treats! During our first few years, customers would often ask if we planned on opening a store one day in addition to our truck. We're happy to be growing, and, yes, to also have a storefront bakery café where you can see us bake and spend some time (and eat lots of treats, of course!).

Please come visit us at both The Treats Truck and The Treats Truck Stop!

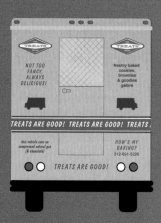

TRUCK:

To find out more about The Treats Truck and to see our truck schedule, go to **www.treatstruck.com** or call **(212) 691-5226**, and follow us on **Twitter @thetreatstruck**.

TRUCK STOP:

To find out more about The Treats Truck Stop, go to **www.thetreatstruckstop.com**. Come by our shop or write to us at **521 Court Street, Brooklyn, NY 11231**, and follow us on **Twitter @treatstruckstop**.

Acknowledgments

There are so many people I want to thank.
From small daily acts of kindness to big ongoing gestures of
generosity, thoughtfulness, and goodwill. So many of you
contribute to make what I do possible. I am forever grateful
and shower the following people with my love and thanks:

My parents, Leslie and **Kenji Ima**, for their incredible love and support (and for happily tackling delivery duty every time they're in town); my brother, **Matt Ima**, for being the best brother and a Treats Truck supporter through the years (and, yes, for making the delivery rounds, too); all my wonderful family and friends for a hundred thousand reasons (like time together, home-cooked meals, and ideas for new specials); my fellow street vendors, who have made my life so much richer; **my customers**, who make every day a pleasure; **anyone who has ever moved their car to make room for my truck**; the late Ellen Stewart, my mentor and inspiration always; **La MaMa, E.T.C.**, and the **Great Jones Rep** (the best test kitchen ever); **The SITI Company**, Sekiya Billman, my dear friend who helped make it all possible; Hoon Lee, my tech wiz and trusted adviser; **Jennifer Niederhoffer** of ImpressMedia, my favorite PR genius and valued friend; **Janice Sloane** for Seders, weddings, and gift boxes of all sizes; **Claire Rich** and Michelle Doll (the talent and the brains of these two, oh my!); **Melissa Vaughan**, Amber Medalla and **my super staff** for extra recipe testing of 1,000 brownies; Diego Cruz for helping take care of my truck, Sugar; **Margaret Palca** of Margaret Palca Bakes for her generosity and friendship; **Leslie Louise "Tiny" Newton** for our Crazy Times Baking sessions and Hobby Club; Michael Newton for tasting all things crazy times; Cathy "Miss Betty" Skillman for being the best friend a truck could ever have; **Magda DeJose** and **Antonio Ramos**; **Duane Boutte**; Kendall Cornell; Onni Johnson; **Soliman Abdelkarim**; Emily Hellstrom, **John Marino**, **Jasper**, and Lyall; the Kleinman family; Janice Goldman Picker; Ralph Picker; **Cory Goldman**; Elizabeth Hajaistron; **Lee Zalban** of Peanut Butter & Co.; **Michael Harlan Turkell**; Betsy Lerner; Doug Quint and Bryan Petroff at the Big Gay Ice Cream Truck; **Mark Thompson, Capalino+Company**; the team at Arcade Creative Group; **Kenneth Shopsin**; David Weber; **Bryan Bantry**; Dina Avalos; Trudi Oothout; Ole Sondresen; **Marzuki Stevens**; **William Dorvillier**; Gary I. Kahn; **Zach Brooks at Midtown Lunch**; Aaron Silverstein, **Saunders & Silverstein, LLP**; Willy Chang, **Chang's Auto** (a prince and the best mechanic ever); **Ernie**, **Jimmy**, and Sylvia Wong, **Shanghai Stainless Product & Design**; Vic Kessler, Jr., Vic Kessler Signs, Ltd.; **Samantha Kahn**, Jacobson Printing; the NYC Food Truck Association; the **Street Vendors Project**; **Elliot Merberg** for his seasoned advice and wonderful support and all the business advisers at SCORE, NYC (scorenyc.org); Martina Pistis, my bookkeeper and guardian angel; Jason Florio and **Helen Jones** for the tremendous photographs; my lovely and talented agent, Erin Hosier at Dunow, Carlson, and Lerner; my truly amazing editor, **Cassie Jones**; **Jessica Deputato**, Liate Stehlik, Lynn Grady, **Tavia Kowalchuk**, Andy Dodds, Shawn Nicholls, **Paula Szafranski**, Mary Schuck, Joyce Wong, **Karen Lumley**, **Ann Cahn** and everyone else at William Morrow/HarperCollins; and last of all, Austyn Stevens!!!, the crazily talented joy to work with brilliant designer of all things Treats Truck (a thousand exclamation marks of thanks!!!). And one more—to everyone old and new who continues to contribute to the life of The Treats Truck and The Treats Truck Stop, I say, thank you very, very much.

INDEX

Note: Page references in *italics* indicate photographs.

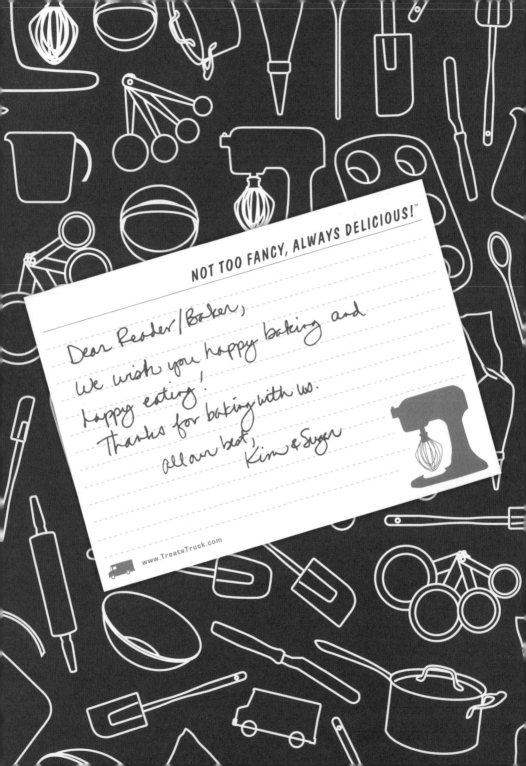

NOT TOO FANCY, ALWAYS DELICIOUS!™

Dear Reader/Baker,
We wish you happy baking and happy eating!
Thanks for baking with us.
All our best,
Kim & Sugar

www.TreatsTruck.com